Ibn al-Jawzee's The Devil's Deception

Edited Translation
by
Dr. Abu Ameenah Bilal Philips

ISBN 1 898649 20 0

British Library Cataloguing in Publication Data.
A catalogue record for this book is available from the British Library.

First Edition, 1417 AH/1996 CE

Cover design: Abu Yahya

Published by: Al-Hidaayah Publishing and Distribution
P.O. Box 3332
Birmingham
United Kingdom
B10 9AW

Tel: 0121 753 1889
Fax: 0121 753 2422

www.al-hidaayah.co.uk

TABLE OF CONTENTS

TRANSLITERATION

In order to provide the non-Arab with a more accurate set of symbols than those in current use, I have adopted a somewhat innovative system of transliteration. However, no transliteration can express exactly the vocalic differences between two languages nor can Roman characters give anything more than an approximate sound of the original Arabic words and phrases. There is another difficulty in romanizing certain combinations of Arabic words which are pronounced differently from the written characters. Included in this category is the prefix "*al*" (representing the article "the") when it precedes words beginning with letters known as *al-Huroof ash-Shamseeyah* (literally 'sun letters'), the sound of "l" is merged into the following letter; for example, *al-Rahmaan* is pronounced *ar-Rahmaan*. Whereas in the case of all other letters known as *al-Huroof al-Qamareeyah* (literally 'moon letters'), the "*al*" is pronounced fully. I have followed the pronunciation for the facility of the average reader by writing ar-Rahmaan instead of *al-Rahmaan* and so on.

Consonants

ء	'		ض	d
ب	b		ط	t
ت	t		ظ	th
ث	th		ع	'
ج	j		غ	gh
ح	h		ف	f
خ	kh		ق	q
د	d		ك	k
ذ	th		ل	l
ر	r		م	m
ز	z		ن	n
س	s		ه	h
ش	sh		و	w
ص	s		ي	y

Vowels

َ	**a**		ـَا	**aa**
ُ	**u**		ـُو	**oo**
ِ	**i**		ـِي	**ee**

The system adopted in the book as as follows:

Shaddah (ّ) - The *shaddah* is represented in Roman letters by doubled consonants. However, in actual pronunciation the letters should be merged and held briefly like the "n" sound produced by the "n" and "kn" combination in the word unknown or like the "n" in unnatural and unnecessary. I have made an exception with (ـِيّ) instead of iyy, I have used *eey* as in *islaameeyah,* because this more accurately conveys the sound in English.

INTRODUCTION TO THE SECOND EDITION

The first edition of this book published under the title *The Devil's Deception of the Shee'ah* has been out of print for more than five years. It was published in 1985 along with *Plural Marriage in Islaam* which has since been reprinted more than four times. I did not reprint *The Devil's Deception* because the Shi'ite propaganda threat to new-Muslims in the West has been significantly reduced. The main cause of that reduction is the recent publication of a number of good books in English which clearly explain the Islamic creed. However, Shi'ite missionary work has again intensified among English-speaking Muslim communities around the world that are ignorant of the history of Shi'ites and tenets of their creed. Spear-heading this attack is *Tahrike Tarsile Qur'an, Inc.,* in Elmhurst, New York. This publishing company reprints popular translations of the Qur'aan by Pickthall and Yusuf Ali to gain credibility among the innocent masses. They also publish M.H. Shakir's Shi'ite translation called, *Holy Qur'an,* along with a variety of anti-Islamic tracts like, *And Then I was Guided, The Right Path,* etc. A major offensive has been launched against indigenous Muslim communities in Philippines, Sri Lanka, and Liberia. Their materials are creating doubts in the minds of young Muslims anxious for the return of Islaam in their various countries. Consequently, a number of Islamic institutions, organizations, individuals and book publishers have impressed on me the need for a reprint of the *Devil's Deception* on numerous occasions over the past five years.

Another translated work on Shi'ism which I did called *Mirage in Iran* was reprinted a couple of years ago, without any revision, by Abul Qasim Bookstore in Jeddah, Saudi Arabia. However, this translation of *The Devil's Deception* has been revised and improved in order to increase its benefit to the readers. One of the unique aspects of the original translation of the *Devil's Deception of the Shee'ah* is the extensive footnotes which I added to increase the historical content and relevance of the work. Though these footnotes are rather cumbersome and at times more than the text itself, they do provide essential background information for the average reader. Consequently, I have kept them, but I have tried to improve the layout to make reading them easier.

It should also be stated that the differences between Islaam and Shi'ism are not only legal and political, but they touch the fundamental principles of faith. The essential difference between true Islaam and Shi'ism lies in the concept of God and man's relationship to God. True Islaam holds that God's attributes are unique to Him alone, while Shi'ism has given some of God's attributes to human beings whom they have titled 'Imaams'. For Shi'ites the Imaams are intermediaries between man and God, and without their intercession humans are lost. As the religion of Islaam brought by Prophet Jesus was changed by men into another religion which they named 'Christianity', the final revelation of Islaam brought by the last Prophet, Muhammad (ﷺ), has been changed by men into another religion which they called 'Shi'ism'.

Dr. Abu Ameenah Bilal Philips

TRANSLATOR'S FOREWORD

Since the Iranian "Revolution" of 1978, there has been a concerted effort to spread the Shee'ah doctrine by force of arms in the Arab world and by propagation and political influence elsewhere - especially in the West. Shi'ite activity in the West has not been directed at non-Muslims to convert them to Shi'ism, but has been directed specifically at Muslims ignorant of Islaam but enthralled by the thought of Islamic revolution. Consequently, the brunt of Shi'ite propaganda has fallen on new-Muslim communities in the Americas where the majority of Muslims are in the formative years of their Islaam. These communities have been flooded with free literature in English filled with historical distortions, lies, and innovations, and many new-Muslims have been given expense paid guided tours of Iran and exposed to the 'fruits of the revolution'.

In the Muslim world a number of refutations of the Shi'ite beliefs have been made by early scholars, and Shi'ite deviations from the mainstream are well known. Also a number of books and pamphlets have been written recently in rebuttal to the Shi'ite's deceptive call to mend the rift between Sunni and Shee'ah. However, due to the extreme scarcity of material in English concerning the history of Shi'ites and their creed, little or no comparison can be made by new-Muslims. They are subsequently overwhelmed by the Iranian propaganda onslaught in which many of the more deviant beliefs have been cleverly disguised. Hence there is a dire need for the translation of authoritative classical works on the Shee'ah. Although classical works written in polemic style tend to alienate readers who are uncommitted to either side of the controversy, such works often contain a wealth of important information.

The work at hand represents an abridged translation of the introduction and four chapters from Ibn al-Jawzee's classic, *Talbees Iblees,*[1] which deals with the Devil's deception of some Muslim

---

[1] Literally "Talbees" means deception. Iblees, the personal name of the Devil is derived, according to Arab philologists, from the root "balasa" because Iblees has nothing to expect (ublisa) from the mercy of God.

scholars, mystics and philosophers as well as deviant psuedo-Islamic sects. Three of the sections concern the birth and development of the sects known collectively as the Khawaarij (Khaarijites), the Shee'ah (Shia or Shi'ites) and the Baatineeyah. The first two are the first deviations from mainstream Islaam, and the third is an offshoot of the Shee'ah.

Any comprehensive study of Shi'ism has to include the Khawaarij, because to a large degree the Shi'ite deviation represents an extreme reaction to the extremes of the Khawaarij. The Khawaarij declared 'Alee ibn Abee Taalib to be a Coffer (disbeliever) and the Shi'ite elevated him and some of his descendants to the leval of demi-gods. Meanwhile mainstream Islaam, often referred to as Sunni Islaam, considers him to be neither a coffer nor a demi-god, but one of the greatest companions of the Prophet (ﷺ)[2], and the fourth of the Righteous Caliphs. No serious historical study of the Shee'ah could be considered complete without a look at what it gave birth to, the ultra-deviant sects of the Baatineeyah.

In the sects of the Baatineeyah, the ideas and philosophy of Shi'ism were projected to their inevitable conclusion, in which 'Alee ibn Abee Taalib and some of his descendants became manifestations of God on earth. The Christian belief that Prophet Jesus was God incarnate, in an even more detestable form, became part of the belief of a people who called themselves Muslims just as the Prophet (ﷺ) had predicted, "*You will follow the ways of the nations before you inch by inch and foot by foot to such a degree that if they entered a lizard's hole, you would go in after them.*" When he was asked if by former nations he meant the Christians and the Jews, he replied, "*Who else could it be*?"[3]

---

[2] The Arabic phrase "Sal-lallaahu 'alayhi wa Sallam" (may Allaah's peace and blessings be upon him), is a prayer which all Muslims are enjoined to say whenever the Prophet's name is mentioned.

[3] Reported by Abu Sa'eed and collected by al-Bukhaaree and Muslim.

In closing, it should be noted that all of the footnotes in the text are mine. Footnotes were added to identify the sources of the *hadeeths* mentioned by the author and to indicate their degree of authenticity where necessary. Extensive footnotes were also added to clarify the background of many of the historical references given by the author.

I hope that this work will be of benefit to all who read it and pray that Allaah accepts it as a good deed done purely for His pleasure.

Abu Ameenah Bilal Philips
March 15, 1985

AUTHOR'S BIOGRAPHY

'Abdur-Rahmaan ibn 'Alee ibn Ja'far al-Jawzee was born in the city of Baghdad in approximately 1114 CE and grew up studying under the leading scholars of his time, including his uncle, Muhammad ibn Naasir al-Baghdaadee, a scholar of *Hadeeth*, *Fiqh* and Arabic grammar.

Ibn al-Jawzee became an outstanding scholar of the twelfth century especially in the Hadeeth sciences for which he was titled *"Al-Haafith"*. He also was noted for his scholarship in the fields of History, Linguistics, Tafseer and Fiqh. In fact, he became the leading scholar of the Hambalee Madh-hab of his time and played a very important role in reviving and spreading it, especially after becoming a favorite of the 'Abbaasid Caliph, al-Mustad'ee (1142-1180 CE). In the year 1179, he had five schools in the capital in which he used to lecture. However, his enthusiasm for his Madh-hab created ill-feeling and jealousies among the other scholars. During the reign of al-Mustad'ee's son, Caliph an-Naasir Lideen-illaah (1159-1225 CE), he was banished to Wasit, where he remained for five years. In the year 1199, he was released and returned to Baghdad, where he died two years later.[4] Ibn al-Jawzee lived to the ripe old age of 87 and was a prolific writer throughout most of his life. Recently, Professor 'Abdul-Hameed al-'Aloojee, an Iraqi scholar conducted research on the extant writings of Ibn al-Jawzee and wrote a reference work in which he listed Ibn al-Jawzee's works alphabetically, identifying the publishers and libraries where his unpublished manuscripts could be found. The number of Ibn-al-Jawzee's books reached a staggering total of three hundred and seventy-six texts. However, even this large number cannot be considered surprising given Ibn al-Jawzee's high regard for time. He was reported to have said, "Many people used to pay me social visits

[4] Ibn al-Jawzee, *al-Misbaah al-Mudee fee Khilaafah al-Mustadee,* (Baghdad, Awqaaf Press, 1976) vol. 1, pp.37-39.

and I likewise until I realized that time is a most noble and precious thing, and hence began to dislike visiting. However, I became caught between two possibilities; if I refused their visits, I would ultimately feeling lonely and miss something which I had grown accustomed to, but if I accepted their visits, my time would be wasted. Consequently, I began to avoid visits to the best of my ability and if it became unavoidable, I would limit my conversation in order to hasten the visit's end. I also prepared work to do during my visits so that no time would pass idly by."

Among the most famous of Ibn al-Jawzee's works in the field of sectarianism is *Talbees Iblees,* from which this abridged translation of four of its chapters was made. In the field of biography of the Sahaabah's and the early generation of scholars is his book, *Sifah as-Safwah,* which consists of three large volumes and *Tareekh 'Umar ibn al-Khattaab,* (Beirut: Daar ar-Raaidal-'Arabee, 1982). His book, *Taqweem al-Lisaan,* (first edition, Cairo: Daar al-Ma'rifah, 1066), was written in the field of Arabic Linguistics. In the field of science of Tafseer, Ibn al-Jawzee wrote a nine volume work entitled *Zaad al-Maseer fee 'Ilm at-Tafseer,* (Damascus: al- Maktabah al-Islaameeyah, 1964), and in Hadeeth *al-'Ilal al-Mutanaahiyah fee al-Ahaadeeth al-Waahiyah,* (first edition, Faisalabad, Pakistan Idaarah al-'Uloom al-Athareeyah, 1979) and *Al-Mawdoo'aat,* (Madeenah, Saudi Arabia: Al-Maktabah as-Salafeeyah, 1966), which consists of three volumes.

AUTHOR'S INTRODUCTION

All praise is due to Allaah, Who only gives the criterion of justice to the most pious among scholars and intellectuals. It is He Who sent messengers bearing glad tidings of reward and warnings of punishment and He also revealed to them divine books containing perfect laws free from any deficiency, blemish, or fault, which explained the wrong and the right.

I praise Him as one who knows that He is the causer of all causes praises Him, and I sincerely testify to His oneness without a trace of doubt. I also bear witness that Muhammad is His slave and messenger whom He sent when disbelief hung like a veil on the face of belief. He removed the darkness with the light of divine guidance, lifted the curtains of ignorance and explained to the people what was revealed for them. He clarified all which was unclear in the Qur'aan and left Muslims in a clear state, free from any distortion. May Allaah's peace and blessings be on him, on all of his family and companions, and on all those who righteously follow in their footsteps until the day of resurrection and judgement.

Surely the greatest God given blessing to humankind is the intellect, because it is the sole instrument by which God, Most Glorious, is known, and the only way by which belief in the Prophet is realized. However since the intellect can't take responsibility for everything humankind requires, messengers were sent and divine books were revealed. That is, the divine law is like the sun and the intellect like the eye which sees the sun, if the eye is open and healthy. When the true message of the prophets is accepted by the intellect after exposure to miraculous proofs, it submits to the prophets and depends on them for understanding the hidden and unseen world.

After blessing the world of man with intellect, Allaah began humankind's earthly existence with the prophethood of Aadam, peace be on him, who taught his descendants according to divine revelation. Humankind remained on the right path until Cain separated himself from the path of righteousness by following his desires and killing his brother. Subsequently, uncontrolled desires split people into factions and drove them into the wilderness of misguidance and the worship of idols. Many contradictory beliefs and practices which were incompatible with the message of the Prophets and confusing to the intellect arose among them. By following their desires, customs, and the influence of their leaders, people confirmed the Devil's wish; that they would all follow him except a handful of believers.[5]

It should be realized that the prophets brought a crystal clear message which they successfully used to confront, the illnesses of society and to effectively cure them according to a common methodology.

However, Satan came and introduced ambiguities into the clear message, mixed poison with the cures, and obscured the straight path by creating around it countless deviant paths. Down through the ages Satan continued to play with people's minds until they fragmented into a multitude of absurd denominations and sects based on despicable innovations. Some eventually worshipped idols in and around the very Ka'bah, the first house of worship built for the worship of the One God, Allaah. The Arabs made certain animals forbidden to themselves like the Saa'ibah, a she-camel left to graze freely; the Baheerah, a Saa'ibah's female offspring whose ear they used to slit; the Waseelah, a sheep which had given birth seven times each time delivering twin females; and the Haamm, a stallion-camel dedicated to the gods according to certain rites. They also buried their baby daughters alive, and deprived orphans of their rightful inheritance etc.

Allaah then sent Mu<u>h</u>ammad, may Allaah's peace and blessings be on him who cancelled these detestable practices and introduced laws for the benefit of mankind. As for his companions, they travelled by the light of his guidance, during his lifetime and after his death, safe from the Devil and his enticements. But when the

---

[5] Soorah al-<u>H</u>ijir 15: 39-40

daylight of their presence faded and the shadows of darkness fell, desires returned, innovations arose and the clear wide path became narrow. Most people split their religion into factions and the Devil rose to the occasion, obscuring, deceiving, embellishing, dividing and fabricating. For, the Devil's deception can only take place in the dark night of ignorance. If the dawn of knowledge rises his deception is easily exposed.

I decided to warn people about Satan's cunning strategies by pointing out his traps because the exposure of evil is a warning against falling into it. In the *Saheehs*[6] of *al-Bukhaaree* and *Muslim* there is a *Hadeeth* related by Hudhayfah in which he said. "People used to ask Allaah's Messenger about the good but I used to ask him about the evil for fear of it catching hold of me."[7] 'Abdullaah ibn 'Abbaas was also reported as saying, "By Allaah, I do not believe there is any one on earth today whom the Devil would like to see dead more than me." When he was asked why that was so, he replied, "By Allaah, when the Devil makes an innovation in the West or the East and a man carries it to me I counter it with a *Sunnah* and it returns to him as he sent it."

Consequently, I wrote this book to warn people against the trials of the Devil. I sought to frighten them by removing the Devil's mask and by exposing his evil tactics. And, Allaah helps everyone who is truthful and whose intentions are wholly sincere.

---

[6] Authentic collections of prophetic traditions.
[7] Collected by al-Bukhaaree.

ADHERENCE TO THE SUNNAH AND JAMAA'AH

'Umar reported that on one occasion Allaah's Messenger (ﷺ) stood up among them and said, "Whoever among you desires the centre of paradise should keep close to the Jamaa'ah (community) for the Devil closely accompanies the solitary individual and is more distant from two."[8]

'Abdullaah reported that on one occasion Allaah's Messenger drew a line in the dust with his hand and said, "This is the straight path of Allaah." Then he drew a series of lines to the right and to the left of it and said, "Each of these paths has a devil at its head inviting people to it." He then recited, "Verily this is my straight path so follow it and do not follow the (twisted) paths.[9]"[10]

'Abdullaah ibn 'Amr reported that Allaah's Messenger (ﷺ) said, "What happened to the children of Israel will surely happen to my nation, step by step. So much so that if there are those who openly have sex with their mothers, among them there will be among my nation those who do that. Surely the Israelites splintered into seventy-two sects and my nation will splinter into seventy-three sects, all of which will be in the fire except one." When the (S̲ah̲aabah) asked "Which sect is it, O Messenger of Allaah?" He replied, "The one followed by my companions and myself."[11]

'Aa'ishah reported that the Prophet (ﷺ) said, "Whoever does something not approved by us will have it rejected.[12]

---

[8] Collected by at-Tirmithee and declared authentic by al-Albaanee in *Saheeh Sunan at-Tirmithee* (no. 1758).

[9] Soorah al-An'aam 6:163

[10] Collected by Ibn Maajah, authenticated by al-Albaanee in *Saheeh Sunan Ibn Maajah* (1/7/11).

[11] Collected by at-Tirmithee and authenticated by al-Albaanee in *Saheeh Sunan at-Tirmithee* (no: 2129).

[12] Collected by al-Bukhaaree (English trans. 3/535-6/861), and Muslim (English trans. 3/931/4266).

Anas ibn Maalik reported that the Prophet (ﷺ) said, "Whoever dislikes my Sunnah is not a true follower."[13]

'Abdur-Rahmaan ibn 'Amr as-Salami said that he heard 'Irbaad ibn Saariyah saying, "Allaah's Messenger (ﷺ) delivered a sermon to us whereby the eyes welled forth tears and the hearts were softened. We said, "Allaah's Messenger, this is a sermon of a person bidding farewell! So what do you enjoin upon us?" He said, "I am leaving you on brightness; its night is (as bright) as its day. None would deviate from it except the one who is doomed to perish. Whosoever survives would see many differences. Then it would be incumbant upon you to adhere to my sunnah and the sunnah of the righteous and pious caliphs, with which yo are familiar. Hold fast to it with your teeth and obedience (to the ruler) is obligatory upon you even if he be an Abyssinian slave. Verily, the (true) believer is like a camel having a (pricking) bridle in its nose. To whichever direction it is driven, it surrenders in submission."[14]

Ibn Mas'ood reported that Allaah's Messenger (ﷺ) said, "I will lead you to the pond (in paradise), and some men will tremble and fall away from me. I will call out, 'O Lord, they are my followers!' So it will be said, 'You do not know what they invented after your passing.'"[15]

Aboo Dardaa reported that Allaah's Messenger (ﷺ) came forth to us while we were sitting making mention of destitution, "Do you fear destitution? By Allaah, in Whose Hands is my life, (the riches of) the world will be poured upon you abundantly, till

---

[13] Collected by al-Bukhaaree (English trans. 7/1-2/1), and Muslim (English trans. 2/703-4/3236).

[14] Collected by Ibn Maajah, authenticated by al-Albaanee in *Saheeh Sunan Ibn Maajah* (1/13-4/41)

[15] Collected by al-Bukhaaree (English trans. 8/378-9/578), and Muslim (English trans. 4/1238/5690).

nothing but this (world) will cause the heart of anyone of you to deviate (from the truth). By Allaah, I am leaving you (after me) with something like brightness, its night and its day are alike." Aboo Dardaa said, "By Allaah, Allaah's Messenger (ﷺ) left us on (a path) like brightness."[16]

Al-Miqdaam ibn Ma'dikarib al-Kindi reported Allaah's Messenger (ﷺ) as saying, "Very soon a tradition of mine will be related to person lying on his couch who will say, 'The Book of Allaah (the Qur'aan) is (enough) between you and us. Whatever we find in it as *halaal* (lawful), we accept it as *halaal* and whatever we find in it as *haraam* (unlawful), we take that as *haraam*.' Behold, whatever Allaah' Messenger (ﷺ) has declared as *haraam* is just like that which Allaah has declared as *haraam*."[17]

'Abdullaah ibn Mas'ood reported on the authority of his father, that Allaah's Messenger (ﷺ) said, "He who deliberately attributes a lie to me, let him take his seat in the Hell-Fire."[18]

Al-Munthir ibn Jareer reported on the authority of his father that Allaah's Messenger (ﷺ) said, "If anyone introduces a good tradition that is followed, he has a reward for that and the reward equivalent to the reward of those who follow it without any dimunition in their own rewards; and if anyone introduces an evil tradition that is followed, its burden as well as the burden of those who act upon it, will lie upon him without any dimunition in their own burdens."[19]

---

[16] Collected by Ibn Maajah and authenticated by al-Albaanee in *Saheeh Sunan Ibn Maajah* (1/6/5).

[17] Collected by Ibn Maajah and authenticated by al-Albaanee in *Saheeh Sunan Ibn Maajah* (1/7/12).

[18] Collected by Ibn Maajah and authenticated by al-Albaanee in *Saheeh Sunan Ibn Maajah* (1/11/28).

[19] Collected by Ibn Maajah and authenticated by al-Albaanee in *Saheeh Sunan Ibn Maajah* (1/40/168).

'Amr ibn 'Awf al-Muzanee reported that the Allaah's Messenger (ﷺ) said, "He who revived a sunnah of mine, then people acted upon it, would earn (a reward) similar to the reward of one who acted according to it; nothing would be deducted from his reward."[20]

'Abul-'Aaliyah[21] reported that the *Sahaabee*, Ubayy ibn Ka'b said, "Adhere to God's path and cling to the Sunnah, for anyone in God's path according to the Sunnah, whose eyes swell up with tears out of piety when remembering Allaah, the Most Merciful, will never be touched by the Hell-fire. Surely a moderate effort in the path of Allaah and the Sunnah is better than great effort in contradiction to them."

Sa'eed ibn Jubayr[22] reported that the Sahaabee ibn 'Abbaas said, "Observing a man from those who adhere to the Prophet's Sunnah, calling others to the Sunnah, and prohibiting innovation, are in themselves worship."

'Aasim reported that Abul-Aaliyah said, "Adhere to the way things were before the early generation became divided." Abu-Ishaaq al-Fazaaree reported that al-Awzaa'ee[23] said, "Patiently restrict yourself to the Sunnah and do not go beyond the limits held by the decisions of the Sahaabah; hold their positions and avoid

---

[20] Collected by Ibn Maajah and authenticated by al-Albaanee in *Saheeh Sunan Ibn Maajah* (1/41-2/173).

[21] His name was Ziyaad al-Barraa, and he was from Basrah. He was among the reliable narrators of Hadeeth from the Sahaabah, his death was in 709CE and Hadeeths narrated by him can be found in both al-Bukhaaree and Muslim. (Ibn Hajar, *Taqreeb at-Tahtheeb,* vol.2, p.443, no.10).

[22] A reliable narrator from the Sahaabah who was born in Kufah. He was killed by the Umayyad general, al-Hajjaaj ibn Yousuf, in the year 713 at the age of about fifty. (*Taqreeb at-Tahtheeb,* vol.1,p.292, no. 133).

[23] 'Abdur-Rahmaan ibn 'Amr al-Awzaa'ee (d.677) was a famous and reliable narrator of Hadeeths as well as a major scholar of Islamic law. (*Taqreeb at-Tahtheeb*, vol.1,p.493, no. 1064).

what they avoided, take the path of your righteous predecessors for verily what was sufficient for them is sufficient for you."

Ubayy narrated that he heard Sufyaan[24] say, "A declaration of faith is meaningless without corresponding deeds: declarations and deeds are only real if based on sincere intentions; and declarations, deeds, and intentions are only correct if they agree with the Sunnah."

---

[24] Sufyaan ibn Sa'eed ath-Thawree (d.681) was a reliable narrator of Hadeeths and a famous scholar of Islamic law. (*Taqreeb at-Tahtheeb,* vol.1, p.311, no. 312).

THE SUNNAH AND BID'AH

If someone argues that eventhough I have praised the Sunnah and criticized Bid'ah, it seems that every deviant innovator in our times claims to be a follower of the Sunnah, I would reply that the word Sunnah literally means a path and there is no doubt that the companions of the Prophet (ﷺ), those who follow in their footsteps, and those who narrated the Prophet's sayings are followers of the Sunnah, because they were on the path where no innovations occurred.

Bid'ah, on the other hand, refers to something which did not exist and was then invented. And, in most cases, innovations conflict with divine law by implying a need for human additions or deletions. Even an invented practice which did not contradict the Sharee'ah or imply any change was disliked by the majority of early scholars. They used to avoid any innovation, even though certain types were allowable, in order to protect the basic principle of Ittibaa', adherence (to the path). For example, when Caliph Abu Bakr and 'Umar asked the Sahaabee, Zaid ibn Thaabit, to collect the Qur'aan in one book, he replied, "How can the two of you do something in the religion which Allaah's Messenger did not do?" 'Abdullaah ibn Abee Salamah reported that when the Sahaabee, Sa'd ibn Maalik, heard two men on Hajj saying, "Labbayk Thal-Ma'aarij (We hear and are coming Oh Owner of the routes of ascent)", Sa'd said, "We never used to say that during the Prophet's time."

Once a man informed the Sahaabee, 'Abdullaah ibn Mas'ood, that a group of people were sitting in the masjid after maghrib and one of them would say, "Say: *Allaahu Akbar*" and the rest would repeat it in unison, than he would say, "Say: *Subhaanallaah*", and they would do likewise, then he would say, "Say: *Al-hamdullillaah*" and they would do so. Ibn Mas'ood told the man to inform him of their whereabouts if he found them doing that again. When he went back to where they were, he sat until he heard them, and he returned to inform Ibn Mas'ood. Ibn Mas'ood went to them and said, "I am

‘Abdullaah ibn Mas‘ood. By Allaah besides who there is no God, you have wrongfully brought an innovation and considered yourselves more knowledgeable than the companions of Muhammad (ﷺ).” ’Amr ibn ‘Utbah[25] said, “I seek forgiveness Allaah!” Ibn Mas’ood said, “Adhere closely to the Prophet’s path, for if you go to the right of it or to the left, you will go far astray.”

Ibn ‘Auf said, “Once when we were with Ibraaheem an-Nakha‘ee,[26] a man came to him and said, “Abu ‘Imraan, pray to Allaah that He makes me well.” I saw his extreme disgust for that written on his face. Ibraaheem then mentioned the Sunnah and his love for it and mentioned what people had innovated and his dislike for it.”

Muhammad ibn Bakr reported that he heard Fudail ibn ‘Iyaad[27] say, “Be cautious whoever sits with one who innovates (Bid‘ah) in religion.” ‘Abdus-Samad ibn Yazeed reported Fudail as saying, “Allaah will cause the deeds of whoever likes one who innovates in religion to be of no value and remove the light of Islaam from his heart.” And on one other occasion, he reported him as saying, “If you see one who innovates coming on the road, take another road. The good deeds of one who innovates are not taken up to Allaah. And whoever helps one who innovates has helped to destroy Islaam.”

---

[25] ‘Amr ibn ‘Utbah as-Salamee from Kufah was a scholar among the Taabee‘oon (students of the Sahaabah) noted for narrations of Hadeeths from Ibn Mas‘ood. He was martyred during the Caliphate of ‘Uthmaan. (al-Khazrajee, *Tath-heeb Tattheeb al-Kamaal,* (Cairo: Maktabah al-Qaahirah), vol.2, p.291, no. 5338 and *Taqreeb at-Tahtheeb*, vol., p. 74.

[26] Ibraaheem ibn Yazeed an-Nakha‘ee (d.715) from Kufah was a major scholar of Islamic law during the era of the students of the Sahaabah. (Taqreeb at-Tahtheeb, vol.1,p.46, no.30)

[27] Fudail ibn ‘Iyaad at-Tameemee (d.803) a famous Hadeeth scholar, noted for his piety, among the students of the Sahaabah’s students. Among his more noted quotations was: “Whoever fears Allaah will not be harmed by anyone and whoever fears others instead of Allaah will not be helped by anyone.” (*Tath-heeb Tahtheeb al-Kamaal,* vol.2, p. 338-9, no.5739).

It is thus, clear that the early generation of Muslims cautiously avoided all innovations which even had the remotest connection to the religion for fear of actually changing the religion to even the slightest degree. However, there were some new practices which did not contradict the Sharee'ah or change it; these practices were allowed. For example, it was reported that people used to pray separately or in small groups during the nights of Ramadaan and Caliph 'Umar ibn al-Khattab joined them together in a single congregation behind the Sahaabee, Ubayy ibn Ka'b. When 'Umar left the masjid and saw them in one group, he said, "This is a good innovation (Bid'ah)." It was good because congregational Salaah was a legal practice in the religion.[28] Whenever a new matter is firmly based on a principle in Sharee'ah it is acceptable. However, any innovation which attempts to complete some aspect of the religion, is wrong because it implies deficiency in the Sharee'ah. And, if the innovation is one which is contradictory to the Sharee'ah, it is even worse.

Thus, it is followers of the Sunnah who adhere to and follow the Prophet (ﷺ) and the followers of Bid'ah are those who invent things in the religion without having any real basis or support. Because of the extreme deviance of their opinions, they hide behind their innovations, while followers of the Sunnah do not hide their opinions. Their positions are obvious, their ideology well known and a good they will have. The two Sahaabees, - al-Mugheerah ibn Shu'bah and Thawbaan, reported that Allaah's Messenger said, "A group of my followers will remain dominant until Allaah's command for the beginning of the final hour reaches them."[29]

---

[28] During the Prophet's time, the Prophet (ﷺ) prayed the night prayers in congregation on three successive nights and then prayed them alone to show that both practices were allowed.

[29] Collected by al-Bukhaaree and Muslim.

THE DEVIL'S DECEPTION OF THE KHAARIJITES[30]

The first and worst of the Khawaarij was Thul-Khuwaisarah. The Sahaabee, Abu Sa'eed al-Khudree, said, " 'Alee ibn Abee Taalib sent some gold ore wrapped in dyed leather[31] from Yemen[32] to Allaah's Messenger, and he divided it up between four people: Zaid al-Khail, al-Aqra' ibn Haabis, 'Uyainah ibn Hisn and 'Alqamah ibn 'Ulaathah.[33] A person among the companions remarked that they had a better claim to the wealth than these people.[34] When this remark reached the Prophet (ﷺ), he said, "Will you not trust me whom the One above the heavens has trusted? Information comes to me from the heavens morning and evening." Then a man with sunken eyes, high cheekbones, a protruding forehead, thick beard and a shaven head stood up and said,"Muhammad! Fear Allaah". The Prophet (ﷺ) turned to him and replied, "Woe be to you. Am I not the person who fears Allaah the most?" The man then walked away and Khaalid ibn al-Waleed jumped up and said "O Messenger of Allaah, shall I not cut off his head?" But the Prophet (ﷺ) said, "Perhaps he observes prayer." Khaalid then said, "Perhaps one who observes prayers says with his tongue what is not in his heart." The Prophet (ﷺ) replied, "I was not commanded to pierce the hearts of people or slit open their bellies." Then he glanced at the man who was walking away and said. "There will arise a people from among the progeny of this man who will recite the Qur'aan, but it will not

---

[30] Arabic: Khawaarij (Sing. Khaarijee - Seceder) this term refers to anyone who openly rebels against the authority of a rightful Muslim leader . (ash-Shahrastaanee, *al-Milal wan-Nihal,* (Beirut: Daar al-Ma'rifah, 2nd ed. 1975), vol. 1, p. 114).

[31] Dyed with *Qaradh*, pods of the Sant tree. (Acacia nilotica:bot), *Hans Wehr Arabic-English Dictionary,* (Spoken Services Inc., 1976), 3rd. ed.

[32] 'Alee was Ameer of Yemen at that time.

[33] One of the transmitters, 'Ammaarah ibn al-Qa'aa, thought that the fourth person might have been 'Aamir ibn at-Tufail.

[34] Who were chiefs from Najd (Eastern Arabia).

go beyond their throats; they will pass through the religion as an arrow passes through its target."[35]

That man was called Thul-Khuwaisarah at-Tameemee and he is considered the first Khaarijee to arise in Islam. The root of his sickness was that he preferred his own opinion over that of the Prophet (ﷺ). If he had waited to hear what the Prophet (ﷺ) had to say, he would have realized that no opinion can be given precedence over that of Allaah's Messenger (ﷺ). And, it was this individual's tribesmen who later rose in arms against Caliph 'Alee ibn Abee Taalib.[36]

When the struggle between Mu'aawiyah and 'Alee became drawn out,[37] Mu'aawiyah's followers raised copies of the Qur'aan

---

[35] Reported by al-Bukhaaree and Muslim (*Sahih Muslim,* translated by 'Abdul-Hamid Siddiqi, Lahore: AH. Muhammad Ashraf, 1976), vol.2, pp.510-1.

[36] During the reign of Caliph Abu Bakr (632-634), the Tameem tribe rallied behind the false prophetess, Sajaah, who arose among them, then joined forces with the false prophet, Musailamah, and rebelled against Islaam.

[37] After the death of Caliph 'Uthmaan (reign 644-656), 'Alee was appointed as the fourth Caliph in Madeenah in June 656. In December of the same year, 'Alee's forces were inadvertently drawn into a clash with the forces of the companions, Talhah, az-Zubayr and the Prophet's wife, 'Aai'shah. Caliph 'Alee then made Kufah his capital and sent replacements for some of the provincial governors. The people of Syria rejected Sahl Ibn Haneef as replacement for Mu'aawiyah who was at that time demanding vengeance for the death of his cousin, 'Uthmaan, before giving an oath of allegiance to 'Alee. Mu'aawiyah did not consider 'Alee's appointment complete since the oath had not yet been given by some of the major Sahaabah like Usaamah ibn Zayd, Sa'd ibn Abee Waqqaas, Ibn 'Umar, Zayd ibn Thaabit, etc. (Ibn Katheer, *al-Bidaayah wan-Nihaayah,* (Beirut: Maktabah al-Ma'aarif Press 3rd. ed., 1974) vol.7,p.227). 'Alee on the other hand, felt that due to the prevailing confusion, the stability of the state had to be reestablished before 'Uthmaan's murderers could be apprehended. This difference of opinion led to the meeting of their forces on the plain of Siffeen, south of ar-Raqqah on the west bank of the Euphrates in July of 657. Skirmishes between the two sides dragged on for weeks in a half-hearted manner, for neither side was anxious to precipitate a full scale battle between Muslims. (*History of the Arabs,* pg. 179-180, *Itmaam al-Wafaa,* (Egypt: al-Maktabah at-Tajaareeyah al-Kubraa, 9th. ed., 1964) pg.211-2 by Muhammad al-Khadaree Bek)

tied to the end of their spears and invited 'Alee's followers to arbitration based on it. They suggested that a man representing each side meet and come to a solution based on the Qur'aan. Both sides agreed to negotiate and Mu'aawiyah's followers sent 'Amr ibn al-'Aas to represent them. When 'Alee's followers chose Abu Moosa to represent them, Alee expressed that he did not think him suitable and suggested Ibn 'Abbaas instead. However, his followers said that they did not want anyone from among 'Alee's relatives, and they sent Abu Moosaa.[38]

The arbitration was subsequently delayed till the month of Ramadaan. During this period, the very validity of men deciding something which lay in Allaah's jurisdiction, was questioned by one of 'Alee's followers by the name of 'Urwah ibn Uthainah[39] who said, "Judgement belongs only to Allaah."

When 'Alee turned his army away from the plain of Siffeen and entered Kufah, about twelve thousand of his followers did not enter the city with him. Instead, they camped at the town of Harooraa[40] and raised their voices in unison reciting the slogan, 'Judgement belongs only to Allaah!' This incident marks the first appearance of the Khawaarij as a sectarian movement. They subsequently appointed Shuaib[41] ibn Rib'ee at-Tameemee as their Ameer for battle, and 'Abdullaah ibn al-Kawwaa al-Yashkaree as their Ameer for Salaah. These Khawaarij were initially very pious and meticulous about the performance of the various acts of worship. However, their belief that they were more knowledgeable than the Prophet's companion, 'Alee ibn Abee Taalib, became the basis of a terrible sickness which afflicted them and led them astray.

---

[38] Abu Moosaa al-Ash'aree had remained aloof of the struggle between 'Alee and Mu'aawiyah and had counselled people not to fight (*al-Bidaayah,* vol.7, p.277)

[39] Actually his name was 'Urwah ibn Jareer and Uthainah was his mother. *See al-Bidaayah,* vol.7, p.278-9.

[40] A village in Iraq near Kufah. These first dissenters were given the name "The Harooreeyah" or "The Muhakkimah" (*al-Milal wan-Nihal,* vol.1.p.115)

[41] Shabath ibn Rib'ee (*Taareekh,* vol.6, p.52)

'Abdullaah ibn 'Abbaas[42] said, "When the Khawaarij broke away, about six thousand of them gathered at a man's estate and agreed to revolt against 'Alee ibn Abee Taalib. During the period of their meetings, a number of people came to 'Alee and informed him that the group was plotting against him. However, 'Alee told his followers not to attack his followers until they attacked him which they would surely do.

One day I came to 'Alee before the mid-day prayer (Salaah ath-thuhr) and said to him, 'O Ameer al-Mu'mineen,[43] may the Salaah sooth you - please allow me to visit the rebels and speak to them. At first 'Alee replied that he feared for my person but he later allowed me to go when I assured him that I was known among them as a person of good character who would hurt no one. I then went and put on my best clothes of Yemenite cloth and my sandals and I went to visit them at mid-day.

When I entered their camp, I found a people whose devotion in prayer the like of which I had never seen. Their foreheads were scarred from continuous and prolonged prostrations, and their palms were calloused like the knees of camels. Their clothes were washed[44] and their faces lined from staying awake all night. When I greeted them, they replied, 'Welcome Ibn 'Abbaas, what has brought you

---

[42] Ibn 'Abbaas was a cousin of the Prophet (ﷺ) and one of his major companions. The Prophet (ﷺ) gave him the title "Turjumaan al-Qur'aan (the interpreter of the Qur'aan)" and his commentary of the Qur'aan is considered to be the most authoritative after that of the Prophet (ﷺ) himself. Caliph 'Alee made him his Ameer over the city of Basrah (*Taareekh al-Umam wal-Mulook,* vol.5, p.224)

[43] Literally: Leader of the Believers. A title first assumed by the second righteous caliph, 'Umar ibn al-Khattaab, and continued by the third Caliph ,'Uthmaan, as well as the fourth, 'Alee.

[44] Ar. "Murahhadah" (Ibn al-Atheer, *an-Nihaayah fee Ghareeb al-Hadeeth wal-Aathar,* (Beirut: al-Maktabah al-Islaameeyah Press, 1st. ed., 1963) vol.2, p.208).

here?' I replied, "I have come from the Muhaajirs[45], the Ansaars,[46] and the Prophet's son-in-law among whom the Qur'aan was revealed. They know its interpretation better than you do." Some of them refused to debate with me on the grounds that I was a Quraishite saying that Allaah, Most Great and Glorious, said, "Yes, they are an argumentative people.[47] However, two or three of them suggested that I speak with them, so I said, "Tell me what you have against Allaah's Messenger's son-in-law, the Muhaajirs, and the Ansaars, among whom the Qur'aan was revealed? There is not a single one of them among you and they know the Qur'aan's interpretation better than you." They replied that there were three points which they had against 'Alee. When I asked them what they were, they said: "One was that 'Alee made men judges in Allaah's affair even though Allaah, Most Great and Glorious, has said, 'Judgement belongs only to Allaah.[48] So what value are men and their decisions after Allaah's statement?" I said, "That is one point and what else?" They replied, "As for the second point, it is that he fought and killed his enemies, yet did not take any captives[49] nor spoils of war. If it was because the enemy were believers, why was it permissible for us to fight and kill them and not make them captives?" I said, "What is the third point?" They replied, "He erased the title *Ameer al-Mumineen* (Leader of the Believers)[50] from himself." If he is not Ameer al-

---

[45] (Literally emigrants) the title given to the Muslims who emigrated from Makkah to Madeenah.

[46] (Literally helpers) the title given to the Muslims of Madeenah who received the Muhaajirs into their homes.

[47] Soorah az-Zukhruf 43:58

[48] Soorah al-An'aam 6:57 and Soorah Yoosuf 12:40, 67

[49] (Ar. Sabee, pl. Sabaayaa) Prisoners of war who may be made slaves. Both 'Alee and Mu'aawiyah forbade taking captives because the enslavement of Muslims is forbidden in Islaam.

[50] During the arbitration between 'Alee and Mu'aawiyah, Amr ibn al-'Aas told the scribe not to write the title "Ameer al-Mumineen" after 'Alee's name saying that he was not their Ameer. One of 'Alee's supporters, al-Ahnaf, insisted that the title be written, but 'Alee told the scribe to erase it.

Mumineen then surely he must be Ameer al-Kaafireen (Leader of the disbelievers). I asked them if they had anything else besides these points, and they replied that these were sufficient. I then said to them, “As for your statement concerning men’s judgement in Allaah’s affair, I will recite for you from Allaah’s book something which will refute your statement. But if I do so, will you retract your position?” When they replied that they would, I said, “Verily, Allaah has relegated to men an area of His judgement whose value is a mere four dirhams, the price of a rabbit, in the verse:

يَٰٓأَيُّهَا ٱلَّذِينَ ءَامَنُواْ لَا تَقۡتُلُواْ ٱلصَّيۡدَ
وَأَنتُمۡ حُرُمٞۚ وَمَن قَتَلَهُۥ مِنكُم مُّتَعَمِّدٗا فَجَزَآءٞ مِّثۡلُ مَا قَتَلَ مِنَ ٱلنَّعَمِ
يَحۡكُمُ بِهِۦ ذَوَا عَدۡلٖ مِّنكُمۡ هَدۡيَۢا بَٰلِغَ ٱلۡكَعۡبَةِ

O Believers, do not kill game in a state of Ihraam (pilgrim dress). If any of you does so intentionally, the compensation is the sacrifice of a domestic animal similar to it[51] near the Ka‘bah according to the judgement of two just men from among you[52]

Also, he relegated to men an area of his judgement concerning a woman and her husband in the verse:

وَإِنۡ خِفۡتُمۡ شِقَاقَ
بَيۡنِهِمَا فَٱبۡعَثُواْ حَكَمٗا مِّنۡ أَهۡلِهِۦ وَحَكَمٗا مِّنۡ أَهۡلِهَآ إِن
يُرِيدَآ إِصۡلَٰحٗا يُوَفِّقِ ٱللَّهُ بَيۡنَهُمَآۗ إِنَّ ٱللَّهَ كَانَ عَلِيمًا خَبِيرٗا

[51] For example if one killed a moose or water buffalo, he would have to sacrifice a cow in Makkah as compensation. If one killed a very small animal, then, according to ‘Alee’s opinion, rabbit could be sacrificed as atonement.
[52] Soorah al-Maa‘idah 5:95

If you fear discord between them, appoint a judge from his family and one from hers to arbitrate. If they wish reconciliation, Allah will make it happen between them. For Allaah is All-Knowing, whose expertise knows no bounds.[53]

I implore you, by Allaah! Is man's judgement to reconcile what is between themselves, and prevent the spilling of blood more excellent than man's judgement over a rabbit and a woman's (family obligations and rights) or not? Which of them is more important?" When they replied that the arbitration was, I asked them if they would retract their objection to 'Alee's agreement to arbitration and they agreed.

I said, "As for your statement concerning 'Alee's fighting without taking captives or spoils of war, it means that you would have taken your mother, 'Aa'ishah, may Allaah be pleased with her, as a captive.[54] By Allaah, if you say that she is not your mother, you have left Islaam and, by Allaah, if you say that you would have made her a captive and made permissible what is permissible in the case of others (i.e. sex), you have left Islaam. You are caught between two grave errors for Allaah, the Most Great Glorious has said:

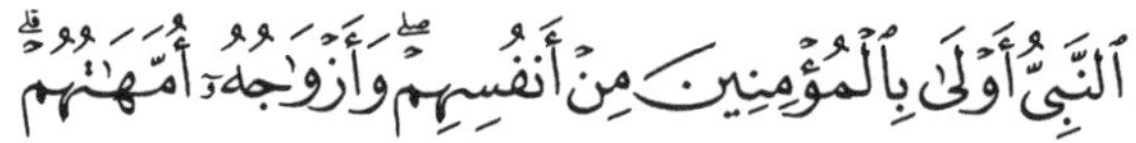

The Prophet is closer to the Believers than their own selves and his wives are their mothers.[55]

---

[53] Soorah an-Nisaa 4:35

[54] She was captured during the battle of the Camel (Dec. 656) and sent home to Madeenah with her brother, Muhammad ibn Abee Bakr as escort, along with all those who fought on her side. (*al-Bidaayah,* vol,p.246).

[55] Soorah al-Ahzaab 33:6

Another group revolted against 'Alee in the following year, and an army was sent to crush the rebellion. However, during the period, 'Abdur-Rahmaan ibn Muljam and his companions met to mourn the loss of their compatriots at Nahrawaan and plan their revenge. They expressed that they could not be content to remain in this world after the passing of their brethren who were unconcerned with being blamed, or rebuked for what they did seeking Allaah's pleasure. It was decided that they would sell their souls to Allaah by seeking out those who they considered leaders of corruption; they would avenge the blood of their brethren, and release Muslims from their clutches.

Muhammad ibn Sa'd reported from his teachers that three Khaarijites, 'Abdur-Rahmaan ibn Muljam, al-Burak ibn 'Abdillaah and 'Amr ibn Bakr at-Tameemee, gathered in Makkah and pledged to kill 'Alee, Mu'aawiyah and 'Amr ibn al-'Aas respectively and not betray one another.[65] Ibn Muljam went to Kufah and on the appointed night when 'Alee left his house to lead the early morning prayers (Salaah al-Fajr), he struck him a vicious blow on the forehead which penetrated to his brain.[66] 'Alee cried out to the people not to let him escape and they caught him. When Umm Kulthoom[67] screamed at him, 'Oh enemy of Allaah, you have killed the Ameer al-Mumineen wrongly, he replied, 'Cry then.' He then went on to say, 'I poisoned my sword, so if he survives me, I pray that Allaah banishes him and destroys him.' So when 'Alee died, Ibn Muljam was brought out to be executed and even though Abdullaah ibn Ja'far cut off both of his hands and feet, he did not cry out or speak. Next both of his eyes were pierced by red hot nails, but he still did not cry out. Instead he began to recite Soorah al-'Alaq: Read in the name of your Lord who created mankind from a leach-like clot - and he finished it while blood flowed from his eye-sockets. How-

[65] At-Tabaree, *Taareekh al-Umam wal-Mulook,* vol.6,p.83.
[66] Ibid., on the 17 th of Ramadaan 661 CE
[67] 'Alee's daughter.

I then asked them if they would retract their objection to 'Alee's refusal to take his defeated Muslim opponents as captives and they agreed.

Then I said, "As for your statement concerning his erasing the title "Ameer al-Mu'mineen", I will give you a similar example concerning someone with whom you are pleased. On the day of Hudaybeeyah[56] the Prophet(ﷺ) made a treaty with the pagans represented by Abu Sufyaan ibn Harb and Suhail ibn 'Amr. He told 'Alee to put it in writing for them, so 'Alee wrote: These are the terms of peace agreed upon by Muhammad, Messenger of Allaah. However, the pagans objected saying, "By Allaah, we do not know you to be a messenger of Allaah, for if we did know you to be so, we would not have fought you." The Prophet (ﷺ) then said, "O Allaah, you know that I am a messenger of Allaah. Erase it, O 'Alee, and write: these are the terms of peace agreed upon by Muhammad ibn 'Abdillaah. By Allaah, surely Allaah's Messenger is better than 'Alee, and he erased a title from himself." Nearly two thousand of the Khawaarij retracted their positions and rejoined 'Alee's forces while the rest of them revolted and were killed."

The Sahaabee, Jundub al-Azdee, said, "When we marched with 'Alee ibn Abee Taalib against the Khawaarij and reached their encampment, to our surprise we heard a loud drone (like the drone of bees) produced by their recitation of the Qur'aan. It was also narrated that when 'Alee agreed to the arbitration, two Khaarijites by the names Zar'ah ibn al-Burj at-Taa'ee and Hurqoos ibn Zubair

[56] Towards the end of the 6th year after Hijrah, the Prophet (ﷺ) and many of his companions donned their Ihraams and headed for Makkah to make 'Umrah. At first the Quraysh vowed not to allow them to enter Makkah, but later they made a ten year truce and demanded the delayal of the Prophet's Umrah until the following year. (Abdus-Salaam Haaroon, *Tahtheeb Seerah Ibn Hishaam,* (Beirut: al-Maktabah al-Amaweeyah, 1972), vol.2, pp.27-33). The truce was known as Sulh al-Hudaybeeyah (the Hudaybeeyah treaty) because it took place at the village of al-Hudaybeeyah on the outskirts of Makkah. (Muhammad ibn Manthoor, *Lisaan al-Arab,* (Beirut: Daar Saadir), vol.1, p.302.

as-Sa'dee,[57] came to visit him and said, "Judgement belongs only to Allaah." 'Alee replied, "Judgement belongs only to Allaah." So Hurqoos said to him, "Repent for your sin and retract your decision to accept human arbitration. Then lead us forth to fight against our enemies until we meet our Lord. If you do not give up human arbitration in the jurisdiction of Allaah's book, I will surely fight you for Allaah's pleasure." The Khaarijites had gathered in the estate of 'Abdullaah ibn Wahb ar-Raasee,[58] who addressed them after thanking and praising Allaah, saying: "It is unbefitting for a people who believe in the Most Merciful (Allaah) and link themselves to the Qur'aan's judgement, that this life, whose love produces only distress, be held dearer than commanding the good, prohibiting evil, and speaking the truth; so join us in rebellion."[59] 'Alee ibn Abee Taalib wrote to them: Surely these two men[60] whom we have accepted as judges have contradicted Allaah's book and followed their desires while we hold our original position. They wrote back to him: Surely you are not angry for your Lord's sake but only for your own . However, if you bear witness to your own disbelief and seek repentance, we will reconsider the disagreement between us, otherwise we will oppose you indiscriminately.

Peace (was-Salaam)

The Khaarijites came across Abdullah ibn Khabbaab[61] during their march and asked him if he had heard any statements from

---

[57] Hurqoos ibn Zuhair, (*Taareekh al-Umam wal-Mulook*, vol.6, p.42, Al-M

[58] Most other sources refer to him as "ar-Raasibee". (*Al-Milal*, vol.1, p.115, *Taareekh al-Umam*, vol.6, p.42. and *al-Bidaayah*, vol.7, p.279)

[59] *Taareekh,* vol.6, p.42

[60] The two arbitrators 'Amr ibn al-'Aas and Abu Moosa decided to annul 'Alee's caliphate (*Taareekh*, vol.6, p.44)

[61] His father, Khabbaab ibn al-Aratt, was a member of the Tameemee tribe who had been captured and sold as a slave in Makkah prior to the advent of Islaam. His mistress, a woman from the tribe of Khuzaam'ah, later freed him and he worked as a swordsmith. Khabbaab was among the first to accept Islaam and he was the first to openly declare his acceptance. He died in Kufah in the year 658 CE.

his father of the Prophet (ﷺ) which he could relate to them. He replied that he had and said, "I heard my father relate from Allaah's Messenger that he mentioned a time of dissension in which one who sits is better than one who stands, one who stands is better than one who walks and one who walks is better than one who runs. And, he said, "If you are alive at that time, be a slave of Allaah who is murdered (than among those who murder)." They then asked him if he really heard his father relate that from Allaah's Messenger and when he replied that he had. They took him to the edge of a river and chopped his head off and his blood flowed in a stream like the lace of a sandal. After that they turned to his pregnant wife, cut open her stomach and spilled its contents.[62] Later, while they were camped in a date palm grove in Nahrawaan, a ripe date fell, and one of them picked it up and tossed it in his mouth. When another person told him he had no right to take it without paying for it, he immediately spat it out of his mouth. One of them sharpened his sword and began to wave it in the air and when the pig of a non-Muslim subject passed by, he slashed it with his sword to try it out. His companions told him that what he did was corrupt, so he found the owner of the pig and gave him a price agreeable to him.[63]

When 'Alee sent a dispatch to the Khaarijites to surrender 'Abdullah ibn Khabbaab's killer, they replied that they all killed him. The demand was repeated three times, and each time they repeated the same answer. 'Alee then told his followers to engage them in battle. During the fighting some of the Khaarijites would say to each other. 'Prepare to meet the Lord going to paradise.' However, they soon suffered a terrible defeat in which 'Abdullaah ibn Wahb and most of his followers were slain.[64]

---

[62] *Taareekh*, vol.8, p.64

[63] Ibid.

[64] This decisive battle took place on the 9th of Safar 658CE and is known in history as "Waq'ah an-Nahr (Battle of the River)" (Mas'oodee, *Murooj adth-Thahab,* iv. 418)

ever, when a section of his tongue was burned, he cried out and when asked why he did so at this point, he replied, 'I hate to die in this world with other than Allaah's remembrance on my tongue.' Looking at the skin on his forehead one could see brownness;the effects of constant prostration in prayer - may Allaah curse him.

When al-Hasan ibn 'Alee wanted to make a peace settlement with Mu'aawiyah, a Khaarijite by the name of al-Jarraah ibn Sinaan revolted against him. Al-Jarraah said to him, 'You have committed shirk as your father did.' Then he stabbed him in his upper thigh.

The Khaarijites continued to rise in revolt against the Muslim state massacring innocent Muslim men, women, and children during both the Umayyad and 'Abbaasid dynasties.[68]

---

[68] Under Caliph Mu'aawiyah's twenty years of administration (660-680), the agitation of the Khaarijites was prevented from seriously breaking out, but he did not succeed in extinguishing it any more than he succeeded in suppressing the feelings and aspirations of the Shee'ah. Several uprisings took place in Kufah and Basrah but were promptly put down. Most of them were in Basrah under the governors, Ziyaad ibn Abeeh and his son 'Ubaidullaah. These insurrections, of which the most formidable was that of Abu Bilaal Mirdaas ibn 'Ubaidah at-Tameemee, settled the tactics of the Khaarijites, whose raids from that period onwards took the from of guerilla warfare and owed their successes mainly to the legendary rapidity of their cavalry. It was only with the great civil war that broke out after the death of Yazeed the first, that the Khaarijite movement assumed serious dimensions and contributed more than anything else to render precarious 'Abdullaah ibn az-Zubayr's hold on the territory that he had at first been able to subdue between the years 683 and 692. Their leaders Abu Taaloot, Najdah ibn 'Aamir, and Abu Fudail captured in succession Yamaamah, Hadramawt, Yaman, and the town of Taif and were only destroyed after the intervention of al-Hajjaaj ibn Yousuf. *(Encylopedia of Islam, p.247)*

A variety of sects soon arose amongst them.[69] For example, the followers of Naafi' Ibn al-Azraq considered themselves pagans as long as they were in a pagan land, but if they left it, they became Muslims. They also considered those who disagreed with their views and those who committed major sins as pagans, while those who did not join their forces during battle were considered as disbeliev-

---

[69] The most infamous of the sects were the Azaariqah, the Ibaadeeyah, and the Sufreeyah. Of these movements, the most dangerous to the unity of the Muslim Empire and the most terrible on account of its ferocity was without doubt that led by Naafi' ibn al-Azraq. The Azaariqah gained temporary control over Kirmaan, Faars, and other eastern provinces and constituted a permanent threat to the security of Basrah and the surrounding country. Only later in 699 did Caliph 'Abdul-Malik's general, Hajjaaj ibn Yousuf finally overcome them and kill the last and most clever of the Azraqee leaders Qataree ibn-al-Fujaa-a. *(Encylopedia of Islam. p.247).* The Ibaadeeyah took their name from 'Abdullaah ibn Ibaad al-Murree at-Tameemee, the most tolerant of the Khaarijite founders of sub-sects. The Khaarijites of the seventh century who originated in Basrah around Abu Bilaal Mirdaas represent the origin of both the Ibaadeeyah and the Hufreeyah.

After the death of Abu Bilaal, 'Abdullaah ibn Ibaad became the leader of the moderates, since in the year 685, he parted from the Azaariqah. Ibn Ibaad and his followers remained in Basrah when the Azaariqh left the city in revolt against the Umayyads and maintained friendly relations with Umayyad Caliph 'Abdul-Malik. The policy of Ibn Ibaad was continued by his successor, Abu Shu'thaa Jaabir ibn Zaid al-Azdee, the chief scholar of the Ibaadeeyah, who came from 'Umman. Abu 'Ubaidah, Muslim ibn Abee Kareemah at-Tameemee, the disciple and successor of Jaabir ibn Zaid was himself an eminent scholar who wrote a compilation of Hadeeths. He also maintained Ibn Ibaad's policy but after the death of Caliph 'Umar ibn 'Abdul-Azeez, favourable conditions for the Ibaadeeyah came to an end as his followers leaned towards revolt. Ibaadite insurrection broke out in several Muslim countries. However, after Abu 'Ubaidah's death (during Mansoor's caliphate), the Ibaadite community of Basrah began to decline. In southern Arabia an Ibaadite revolt broke out in 747 which not only wrested Hadramaut and San'a from the Umayyad's but also spread to Makkah and Madeenah for a time. In the year 748 the Ibaadites were finally defeated near Wadi al-Quraa. Today the Ibaadeeyah is the religion of the main branches of the Ghaafiree and Hanaawee clans in 'Umaan. They are also to be found in Zanzibar, Persia. Algeria, and Libya. The Ibaadites did not consider non-Khaarijites disbelievers and they allowed marriage with non-Ibaadites. *(Encyclopedia of Islam, pp 143-4, Al-Milal vol. 1, pp.* 118-137.

ers. They made the killing of Muslim women and children allowable as they adjudged them pagans. However, one of the Azraqees, Najdah ibn 'Aamir ath-Thaqafee, diverged from some of Naafi's views and prohibited the spilling of Muslim blood or the taking of Muslim property. He also held that sinners among his followers would be punished in a place other than the hell-fire and that hell was reserved for those who disagreed with his sectarian views.

Some of the Khaarijite sects used to hold that anyone who consumed as little as two pennies[70] of an orphan's wealth would go to hell, because Allaah, Most Great and Glorious has promised the fire for those who commit this error.[71] Also among the beliefs of the Khaarijites is the opinion that the Imaamate (leadership of state) is not specific for anyone unless he is knowledgeable and pious, and anyone from the common people who has both these qualities can be the Imaam.[72] From their opinion arose the views of the Mu'tazilah concerning judging good and evil by the intellect, and that justice is whatever the intellect judges to be just.[73]

The strange beliefs of the Khaarijite sects and the recorded accounts of their activities are numerous, and I do not feel that further elaboration is necessary considering the fact that the main intention of this chapter is a look at the tricks and strategies of Iblees; how he deceived those fools who showed their ignorance by their actions and their beliefs that 'Alee ibn Abee Ṯaalib and those with him from among the Muhaajirs and the Anṣars were in error while they were correct. They made permissible the spilling of the blood of children while forbidding the eating of a date without paying its

---

[70] The word used in the original is Fals (pl. Fuloos) - a small coin in Iraq and Jordan equal to one thousandth (0.001) of a dinar.

[71] This is in reference to Soorah an-Nisaa (4) verse 10: "Those who unjustly consume the property of orphans, only consume fire into their bellies, and they will enter a blazing fire."

[72] This is in opposition to the position of the Sunnee Muslims, who follow the Prophet's statement related by Abu Bakr, "The Imaams should be from the Quraish tribe."

[73] *Al-Milal,* vol.1, p.113.

price. They greatly exerted themselves in worship, staying up all night in prayer, and when his tongue was cut Ibn Muljam cried out because he would miss the opportunity to mention Allaah's name. Yet, they made permissible the murder of 'Alee ibn Abee Taalib, may Allaah enoble him, and unleashed their swords on the Muslims.

I am not surprised at their certainty about their knowledge nor their conviction that they were more knowledgeable than 'Alee, may Allaah be pleased with him, for Thul-Khuwaisarah had told the Prophet of Allaah (ﷺ), 'Be just, for you have been unfair.' And, it was Iblees who led them to perpetrate these infamies; we seek refuge in Allaah from abandonment and defeat (at the hands of Iblees).

Muhammad ibn Ibraaheem reported that he heard Allaah's Messenger say, "There will arise a people among you who will regard your prayers, fasting and good deeds with contempt and scorn; they will recite the Qur'aan, but it will not go past their throats, and they will pass through the religion the way an arrow passes through its prey." [74] 'Abdullaah ibn Abee Awfaa[75] reported that the Prophet of Allaah said, 'The Khaarijites will be the dogs of hell's inhabitants.

[74] Collected by al-Bukhaaree and Muslim.

[75] His father's name was 'Alqamah ibn Khaalid al-Aslamee, and both he and his father were companions of the Prophet (ﷺ). Hadeeths narrated by him can be found in all of the Six books and he was the last Sahaabee to die in Kufah (706CE). *Taqreeb at-Tahtheeb*, vol. p.402. no. 193.

THE DEVIL'S DECEPTION OF THE SHEE'AH[76]

Just as Iblees succeeded in deceiving the Khaarijites into fighting 'Alee ibn Abee T̲aalib, he also succeeded in making others go to extremes in their love for 'Alee.

---

[76] The term Shee'ah (pl. Shiya') comes from the verb "Shaa'a" which means to spread. Hence Shee'ah means a faction or sect and is used with that meaning in the Qur'aan in both singular and plural forms many times. For example, "Then We will certainly drag out from every sect (Shee'ah) those who were most obstinate in their rebellion against (Allaah) Most Gracious." (Soorah Maryam 19:69) and "As for those who divide their religion and break up into sects (Shiya') you have no part in them in the least. Their affairs are with Allaah: He will tell them the truth of what they did in the end." Soorah al-An'aam 6:159). The term was first used to describe both 'Alee's followers (Shee'ah 'Alee) as well as those of Mu'aawiyah (Shee'ah Mu'aawiyah). However, after 'Alee's death and Mu'aawiyah's nomination, 'Alee's followers retained the name exclusively and Mu'aawiyah, his descendants, and followers were known as the Umayyads, because he was from the Umayyah clan.

After the murder of Caliph 'Alee ibn Abee T̲aalib in January, 661 CE and his secret burial at Najaf, his son al-H̲asan was declared Caliph by the people of Iraq. Al-H̲asan, however, abdicated in favor of Mu'aawiyah for a guaranteed subsidy and pension which he himself fixed and retired to Madeenah. When he died at the age of forty-five (669CE), his brother al-H̲usayn became the focal point of 'Alee's followers during the rest of Mu'aawiyah's reign. On Mu'aawiyah's death (650 CE), al-H̲usayn refused to acknowledge the Caliph's son and successor, Yazeed, and decided to respond to the urgent and reiterated appeals of the Iraqis to rebel. However, before doing anything, he resolved to test how matters stood by using his cousin, Muslim ibn 'Aqeel. When Muslim arrived, the Shee'ahs rushed to swear fidelity to al-H̲usayn, so Muslim wrote to his cousin in Makkah to come and take charge of the movement. Against the advice of his other relatives in Madeenah, al-H̲usayn,with his immediate family, set out for Kufah from Makkaah where he had sought refuge after refusing to swear fealty to Yazeed. In the meanwhile, 'Ubaidullah ibn Ziyaad, appointed governor of Iraq, entered Kufah with little resistance from the Kufans and executed Muslim. Not far from Kufah, al-H̲usayn learned of his cousin's fate but continued toward Kufah until he and his band which had dwindled to about two hundred souls were surrounded by 4,000 troops under the command of 'Umar, the son of Sa'd ibn Abee Waqqaas, the famous S̲ah̲aabee and general. At Karbalaa, about twenty-five miles northwest of Kufah, upon their refusal to surrender they were massacred. The Prophet's (ﷺ) grandson fell dead on the 10th of Muharram (October 10, 680CE), and his head was severed and sent to

Among the extremists were some who claimed that 'Alee was God, while others claimed that he was better than the Prophets. Some of the extremists considered it a religious duty to curse Abu

---

Caliph Yazeed in Damascus. The Caliph deplored this horrible ending which he had neither desired nor ordered His instructions had been to secure the person of al-Husayn, to prevent him from prolonging a dangerous agitation. He gave the head back to al-Husayn's sister, Faatimah and son, 'Alee, Zain al-'Aabideen, who buried it with the body in Karbalaa. Yazeed treated the 'Alids who survived with honor, providing generously for their needs and gave them an escort back to Madeenah. *(Encyclopedia of Islam, p.142, Taareekh, vol.6, pp.262-6).*

However, the blood of al-Husayn, even more than his father, proved to be the seed of the Shee'ah sect. The passion factor of martyrdom took on major proportions among the so-called followers of 'Alee. Their anguish at al-Husayn's betrayal led them even to claim that al-Hasan was poisoned on Mu'aawiyah's orders, and vengeance for al-Husayn became their battle-cry. *(History of the Arabs, p.190)*

A group of the Shee'ah under Sulaymaan ibn Surad armed themselves vowing to fight to death against the Umayyads by doing penance at al-Husayn's grave four years after the battle of Karbalaa. They hoped to atone for the guilt which they had brought upon themselves for having not fought for or died with the dead al-Husayn. In commemoration of al-Husayn's martyrdom, the Shee'ah have established the practice of annually observing the first ten days of Muharram as days of lamentation, and have developed a passion play called Ta'ziyah about his struggle and suffering. This annual passion play is enacted in Iraq in two parts, one called 'Aashoora (the tenth day) in al-Kaathimayn (close to Baghdad) in memory of the battle and the other forty days after the tenth in Karbalaa entitled "Return of the Head". In popular language Ta'ziyah refers to a copy of al-Husayn's tomb at Karbalaa often elaborately carved and exhibited in the ceremonies of mourning for al-Husayn. The plays in Iraq and elsewhere include street processions such as a cavalcade with al-Husayn's house, the marriage procession of al-Hasan's son, al-Qaasim, and al-Husayn's daughter, Faatimah, by his Persian wife, Shahrabaanoo (daughter of Yezdegird III), the procession to the cemetery with the coffin, and self-flagellation by both participants and spectators. *(Encyclopedia of Islam, pp.590-1)*

From the death of al-Husayn onwards, the Imaamate of 'Alee's progeny became as much of a dogma in the Shiite creed as that of the prophethood of Muhammad (ﷺ) in Islaam. The Imaam became the sole legitimate head of the Muslim community divinely designated for the supreme office; a spiritual and religious leader as well as a secular one, endowed with a mysterious power transmitted to him from his predecessor. As such he stands far superior to any other

Bakr and 'Umar, while others declared that Abu Bakr and 'Umar were disbelievers.There were so many other ridiculous and absurd sects which arose from among those who went to extremes in their love for 'Alee that much time would be exhausted in trying to mention all of them. Consequently, I will only refer to a few of them.

'Abdul-Waahid ibn Burhaan al-Asadee reported that Is-haaq ibn Muhammad an-Nakha'ee al-Ahmar used to say that 'Alee was Allaah. Also, he said that in Madaa'in there was a group of extrem-

---

human being and enjoyed infallibility ('Ismah). The Imaamate, thus, became and has since continued to be the main differentiating element between Sunnites (orthodox) and Shiites.

The Shee'ah took its final shape under the 'Abbaasids but they fared no better under this regime than under the Umayyad, in spite of the fact that they had been an important factor in establishing the former at the expense of the latter. During the reign of Abu Ja'far al-Mansoor (754 -75) the revolt of the disgruntled Shee'ah, headed by Ibraaheem and Muhammad an-Nafs az-Zakeeyah, great grandsons of al-Hasan, was ruthlessly crushed. Muhammad was killed and gibbeted (December, 6, 762CE) in Madeenah; Ibraaheem was decapitated (February 14, 763CE) near the unruly Kufah and his head dispatched to the Caliph. (*Taareekh,* Tabaree, vol.iii, pp.245-65, 315-16). Things improved under al-Ma-moon (813-833), who even went as far as to don their color, green, and proclaim as their apparent Alee ar-Ridaa, one of their Imaams.Yet this was of no permanent avail for soon came al-Mutawakkil (847-861) who in 850CE resumed the early practice of persecuting the Shee'ah; he destroyed the tombs of 'Alee at Najaf, and the more venerated one of al-Husayn at Karbalaa,(*Murooj,* al-Mas'oodee, vol. vii, pp.302-3); thereby earning the everlasting hatred of all Shiites. This general hostility led the Shiites to adopt the principle of dissimulation (Taqeeyah - literally "caution or fear") , i.e. dispensation from the requirement of religion under compulsion or threat of injury. The legitimacy of Taqeeyah as an ethical principle had already been recognized by some Khaarijites *(Al-Milal wan-Nihal,* Shahrastaanee (Beirut: 1975), pp.92,93), but the Shiites made it a fundamental tenet.

In Persia, the Twelver Shee'ah was established in 1502CE by the Safawids, who claimed descent from the seventh Imaam, Moosaa al-Kaathim *(History of the Arabs, p.441).* On his ascension,the founder of the Safawid state, Shaah Ismaa'eel, declared Shiism the state religion of Persia. He gave formal orders to the Imaams of Adharbaijaan to preach the sermon (khutbah) in the name of the twelve Imaams, and then to the Mu-ath-thins to add the Shee'ah formula: I testify that 'Alee is the Walee (friend) of God." The troops were also ordered to put to death any objectors. *(Encyclopedia of Islam, p.188).*

ists (Ghulaah) known as Is-haaqites, who linked themselves to him.[77]

In a book by Abu Muhammad al-Hasan ibn Yahyaa an-Nawbakhtee[78] written in refutation of their extremist views, al-Khateeb reported that after the author mentioned their various claims, he wrote: Among those who became purely insane in extremism in our times was Is-haaq ibn Muhammad known as al-Ahmar. He used to claim that 'Alee was Allaah, Most Great and Glorious, and that he appears all the time.[79] One time Allaah appeared as al-Hasan and at another time as al-Husayn, and it was he in the from of Jibreel,who delegated Muhammad (ﷺ).

A group of the Shee'ah believed that Abu Bakr and 'Umar were disbelievers, and some claimed that they apostated after the Prophet's (ﷺ) death. Others insisted on a declaration of one's innocence from all the Caliphs except 'Alee from whoever disagreed with 'Alee's right to be Imaam. When Zayd refused, they rejected

---

[77] *Al-Milal wan-Nihal*, vol, pp.188-9

[78] A major Shiite theologian and his book was: *Firaq ash-Shee'ah*

[79] The first record of deification of 'Alee came from the enigmatic 'Abdullaah ibn Saba a Yamanite Jew, who converted to Islaam during the Caliphate of 'Uthmaan and entrenched himself among the followers of 'Alee ibn Abee Taalib. Ibn Saba played a significant role in the uprising which started in Kufah amongst 'Alee's supporters and flared up in Egypt. From this rebellion rebels were sent to Madeenah in April 656CE. They surrounded Caliph 'Uthmaan's house and stormed it killing the Caliph. 'Alee and Talhah, az-Zubayr and 'Aai'shah to avoid any bloodshed were being concluded in December 656, Ibn Saba and his cohorts instigated a clash between their forces by simultaneously attacking both sides at night which led to the Battle of the Camel outside Basrah, in which the great companions of the Prophet, Talhah and az-Zubayr, were killed along with many Muslims. Also, it was 'Abdullaah ibn Saba and his band who first attributed divinity to 'Alee ibn Abee Taalib. 'Alee had most of them executed by burning them alive; however, Ibn Saba escaped and was banished from Iraq, where caliph 'Alee and his followers were based. (al-Ash'aree, *Maqaalaat al-Islaameeyeen,* vol.1, pp.50-1, 58-9).

him, and became known as the Rejectors (Raafidah).[80] Among them were those who conferred the Imaamate on Moosa ibn Ja'far, then his son 'Alee, then Muhammad ibn 'Alee ibn Muhammad, then to al-Hasan ibn Muhammad al-'Askaree, and finally to his son, Muhammad the twelfth Imaam; the awaited Imaam, whom they claim did not die, but will return in the last days to fill the earth with justice.

Abu Mansoor al-'Ijlee claimed that Muhammad ibn 'Alee al-Baaqir would return, and that he was his Caliph. He claimed that Allaah had lifted him (i.e. 'Ijlee) up into the heavens and wiped His hand on his head, and he also claimed that he was the Kisaf or Kisf

---

[80] Zayd ibn 'Alee was the first to try to wrest the Caliphate from the Umayyads by armed rebellion after the catastrophe at Karbalaa, when he placed himself at the disposal of the Kufans as their Imaam. After spending a year making secret preparations, he came forward openly, but was killed in street-fighting in the year 740 CE.

After Imaam Zayd's death, the Zaydeeyah took part in several 'Alid uprisings but were not a divided body. They only became a united community when 'Alid, claimants to the Imaamate themselves, took over the spiritual leadership. This was the work of essentially two men: 1. al-Hasan ibn Zayd, founder of a Zaydee state in the south of the Caspian Sea around the year 864, and 2. al-Qaasim ar-Rassee ibn Ibraaheem Tabaatabaa (d.860). On the Caspian Sea about twenty Imaams appeared from al-Hasan ibn Zayd's group at irregular intervals down to about 1126CE after which the Zaydees became merged in the little sect of Nuktawees. The founder of the Zaydees state in Yaman was Yahyaa ibn al-Husayn, grandson of al-Qaasim ar-Rassee. It has survived all the kingdoms of Yaman and remains the major madh-hab of the people of Yaman. The sect is Mu'tazilee in theology and rejects mysticism. In worship it has certain sectarian features in common with other Shiites: the addition of Hayya ilaa Khair al-'Aa'maal (Come to the best of works) to the call to prayer, the prohibition of meat killed by non-Muslims. In family law they prohibit marriage with Christians and Jews. However, they do not allow Mut'ah (temporary marriage) alike the other Shiite sects. In fact their Fiqh is very similar to the Sunni Hanafee school of law. They also recognize the three righteous Caliphs before 'Alee and do not consider the majority of the Sahaabah apostates. (Abu Zahrah, *Taareekh al-Mathaahib*, vol.2, pp.479-516, Encylopedia of Islam, pp.631-2) (piece), which would fall from the sky.[81]

Similarly, another group among the Raafidite Shee‘ah called the Janaahites (Janaaheeyah), who were followers of ‘Abdullaah ibn Mu‘aawiyah ibn ‘Ja‘far Thil-Janaahain, claimed that God's spirit travelled down through the loins of the Prophets and Saints until it reached ‘Abdullaah Thil-Janaahain who did not die and whose return is awaited.[82] There was also a group called the Ghuraabites (Ghuraabeeyah), who claimed that ‘Alee shared a part of prophethood and yet another called the Mufawwidites (Mufawwidah) professed the belief that after Allaah created Muhammad, He delegated the creation of the world to him. A group among them called Thammaamites (Arabic- Thammaameeyah, lit.,

---

[81] This is in reference to verse 9 of Soorah Saba, in which Allaah says: "If We could cause the earth to swallow them up or cause a piece (Kisaf) of the sky to fall on them." Or in reference to verse 44 of Soorah at-Toor, in which Allaah says: "Were they to see a piece (kisf) of the sky falling on them, they would say, 'It is only clouds gathered in heaps.' His followers were called the Mansooreeyah. During the reign of Caliph Hishaam ibn ‘Abdul-Malik (724-43CE), the governor of Iraq, Yousuf ibn ‘Umar ath-Thaqafee, came to know about Abu Mansoor's activities in Kufah and executed him. (*Al-Milal wan Nihal,* vol.1, pp.178-9 and al-*Fisal*, vol.4, p.185).

[82] ‘Abdullaah ibn Mu‘aawiyah's great grandfather, the Sahaabee and the Prophet's cousin, Ja‘far ibn Abee Taalib, was nicknamed Thul-Janaahayn (the possessor of two wings). ‘Abdullaah ibn Mu‘aawiyah also claimed that he was a prophet and later that he was God incarnate and his followers worshipped him. They also used to deny the resurrection, claming that this world was eternal and claimed also that the obligatory rites of Islaam were merely symbolic of certain descendants of the Prophet (ﷺ) to whom allegiance must be given. ‘Abdullaah and his follower revolted against the government in Kufah in the era of the last Umayyad Caliph, Marwaan ibn Muhammad (744-750CE). The Ameer of Kufah fought them until they requested a truce and left Kufah. However they, went and conquered Halwaan, Hamthaan, Rayy, and Isfahan and ruled them until Abu Muslim al-Khuraasaanee, the major ‘Abbaasid propagandist, came and defeated them.

After ‘Abdullaah ibn Mu‘aawiyah's death, his followers claimed that he did not die but was alive in the Isfahan mountain, and that he would remain alive until he reappeared to them. (Al-Ash‘aree, Abul-Hasan, *Maqaalaat al-Islaameeyeen,* (Cairo: Maktabah an-Nahdah al-Misreeyah, 2nd.ed., 1969), vol.1, pp.67-8).

the criticizers) criticized Jibreel because they felt he was commanded to descend upon 'Alee but descended upon Muhammad.[83] Some of the Shee'ah also claimed that Abu Bakr wrongfully denied Faatimah her inheritance.[84] In fact, once after as-Saffaah[85] delivered a speech, an 'Alawite stood up and said, "I am among 'Alee's descendants, may Allaah be pleased with him, O Ameer al-Mumineen, help me against those who have wronged me." When he asked the 'Alawite who wronged him, he replied "I am one of 'Alee's grandchildren and the one who wronged me was Abu Bakr when he took the oasis of Fadak[86] from Faatimah." As-Saffaah asked him whether Abu Bakr

---

[83] For more details see al-Baghdaadee, *al-Farq bain al-Firaq, pp.250-1*

[84] To this day this claim is raised by the Shee'ah during their missionary work among Sunni Muslims.

[85] Caliph Abul-'Abbaasid (750-754CE), the first of the Abbaasid Caliphs called himself as-Saffaah (the bloodshedder) as an ominous warning to his opponents.

[86] Fadak was an oasis town near Khaibar which the Prophet (ﷺ) had received as Fay (war spoils taken without a fight) and it remained in his possession during his lifetime. After his death 'Alee said that the Prophet (ﷺ) had given it to his daughter, Faatimah, her son, and the Prophet's uncle, al-'Abbaas ibn 'Abdul-Muttalib. Caliph Abu Bakr ruled that it could not be inherited. After Abu Bakr's death, Caliph 'Umar allowed al-'Abbaas and 'Alee to take benefit from the oasis town, but did not allow them to own it. ('Abdul-Qaahir al-Baghdaadee, *al-Farq bain al-Firaq*, (Beirut: Daar al-Ma'rifah), pp.16-17).

'Aa'ishah reported that Faatimah sent asking Abu Bakr for her inheritance from what Allaah had given the Prophet (ﷺ) as Fay, Sadaqah (charity) in Madeenah, the oasis of Fadak and the remainder of the Khumus (one-fifth) of the war spoils turned over to the Prophet (ﷺ) from the battle of Khaibar. Abu Bakr replied, "Allaah's Messenger said, 'What we Prophets leave behind is charity and not inheritance. Muhammad's family may take from it, but no more than they need.' By Allaah, I will not change the status of the Prophet's Sadaqah but will keep them as they were in the Prophet's lifetime and dispose of them as Allaah's Prophet did." 'Alee then exclaimed, "I testify that there is no god but Allaah and that Muhammad is His Messenger.' Then he added, "O Abu Bakr, we acknowledge your good qualities. "Then 'Alee mentioned their relationship to the Prophet (ﷺ) and their rights. Abu Bakr replied, "By He in whose hands lies my soul, I love to do good to the relatives of Allaah's Messenger more than I do to my own relatives." (Muhmmad Muhsin Khan, *Sahih al-Bukhaaree,* (Madeenah: Daar al-Fikr), vol.5, pp.49-50, chapter 13, Hadeeth no. 60).

continued to perpetrate this wrong, and he replied that he had. Then he asked him who took charge after Abu Bakr and he replied, "'Umar." So he asked him if he also continued the wrong and he replied that he had. He then asked him who took charge after 'Umar, to which he replied, " 'Uthmaan." Again he asked him if he also continued the wrong and he replied that he had. Then he asked him who took charge after 'Uthmaan." and he began to look around here and there to find a place where he could hide.[87]

Ibn 'Aqeel said that it is obvious that those who formed the Raafidite intended an attack on the foundation of religion and prophethood. For what Allaah's Messenger brought is something from the past not experienced or witnessed by us and we can only be sure about what has been conveyed to us if we believe that it was conveyed by the righteous and knowledgeable among the early generation of Muslims (i.e. the Sahaabah). It is as if we understand only what those, whose practice of the religion and intelligence we have confidence in, understood on our behalf. So if someone were to say that the first thing the Sahaabah did after the Prophet's death was to oppress his family by depriving them of the Caliphate and their inheritance, this could only be a result of the Sahaabah's disbelief in the Prophet (ﷺ).[88] For, correct belief, especially about the Prophets, necessitates the protection of their laws after their deaths; especially those concerning their families and their descendants. Hence if we accept the Raafidites claim that the Sahaabah made these things permissible after the Prophet's death, our confidence in the Sharee'ah would be lost. Because there is nothing between us

---

[87] 'Alee took charge after 'Uthmaan and he did not rectify this supposed wrong. So, either 'Alee continued the oppression of himself and his family or Abu Bakr was right in not giving Faatimah the oasis of Fadak based on the Prophet's (ﷺ) statement that what Prophets leave behind is charity and not inheritance.

[88] According to Shee'ah accounts only three of the Sahaabee, Salmaan al-Faarisee, Abu Tharr, and al-Miqdaad ibn al-Aswad al-Kindee, championed 'Alee's succession on the death of the Prophet (ﷺ) and, therefore, did not fall away from the faith. The other companions of the Prophet (ﷺ) are credited by the majority of the Shee'ah with apostasy for giving the oath of allegiance to Abu Bakr.

and the Prophet (ﷺ) besides what the Sahaabah conveyed and our confidence in them. So if the sum total of what happened to them after the Prophet's death makes us doubt what they conveyed and destroys our confidence in following their reasoned decisions which we have relied upon, it could also be that they did not narrate certain compulsory aspects of the religion, but instead they related only what was in their material interest. That is, they abandoned the Sharee'ah after the Prophet's (ﷺ) death and only a few of his family members continued to follow the religion. With that, beliefs would fall and souls would become too weak to accept any narrated information from the early generations and would find it difficult to accept the very Qur'aan[89] itself.

The extreme "love" for 'Alee caused the Raafidites to fabricate a number of Hadeeths concerning 'Alee's great merit; most of which would be painful for him to hear. A large number of such Hadeeths can be found in the book, *Al-Maudoo'aat.*[90] Among them, for example, is the Hadeeth in which it was reported that the sun set before 'Alee could pray Salaah al-'Asr so it was caused to rise again so that he could make the prayer on time. This Hadeeth is considered false due to its chain of narrators who were all unreliable. It is also considered false due to its content as the time for 'Asr had passed, hence the return of the sun would be considered a new sunrise and not a return of 'Asr time. Similarly, they fabricated a narration that Faatimah took a ghusl,[91] then died leaving a will that her body should not be bathed after her death. It is a lie relative to

---

[89] Famous and respected Shiite scholar from Najaf, Mirza Husain ibn Muhammad at-Tabarsee wrote the book: *Fasl al-Khitaab fee Ithbaat Tahreef Kitaab Rabb al-Arbaab* (A Decisive Statement concerning proof of the Alteration of the Lord of Lord's Book i.e. Qur'aan) in the year 1865 CE. In it he compiled hundreds of texts written by Shiite Scholars in different ages alleging that the Qur'aan is incomplete. (Muhibbuddeen *al-Khateeb, al-Khutoot al-'Areedah,* (Canada: Majlis al-Haq, 1st. ed. 1983) p.4).

[90] By the author himself (Madeenah, Saudi Arabia: al-Maktabah as-Salafeeyah 1966), three volumes.

[91] A complete bath according to Islamic rules.

its chain of narration, and it is ignorant relative to its meaning. The ghusl of the dead body is for the state of impurity produced by death, so how could it be done prior to death.

The Raafadites also have a number of invented Fiqh (legal) rulings which have no basis in the religion, and which contradict the consensus of the early generations of Muslims. The Fiqh issue recorded by Ibn 'Aqeel which he quoted from *Kitaab al-Murtadaa* which says that sujood (prostration in prayer) is not allowed on other than the earth's surface or its natural plant or mineral products. Therefore sujood is not allowed on wool, leather, or hair mats . They also forbade Salaah al-Jamaa'ah (congregational Salaah) based on the stipulation that the Imaam has to be infallible (Ma'soom).

Iblees not only caused them to invent these baseless rulings but deceived them into considering the cursing of the Prophet's companions an article of faith. However, in the two Saheehs[92] the Prophet's command, "Do not curse my companions for verily, if one of you gave (in charity) the weight of Mt. Uhud in gold, it would not equal a handful of what they gave, nor even half a handful"[93] renders this article of faith baseless. 'Abdur-Rahmaan narrated from his father, Saalim, from his grandfather, 'Abdullaah ibn 'Uwaim, who reported that the Prophet (ﷺ) said, 'Verily, Allaah chose me, chose companions for me, and made them my assistants and in-laws. So whoever curses them, is cursed by Allaah, the angels, and all of humankind and on the day of resurrection Allaah will not accept neither their compulsory religious duties nor voluntary ones.[94]

---

[92] Saheeh al-Bukhaaree and Saheeh Muslim.

[93] Reported by Abu Hurayrah and Abu Sa'eed and collected by al-Bukhaaree, Muslim, Abu Daawood, at-Tirmithee, and Ahmad. Wensinck, A.J., and Mensing, J.P. *Concordance,* (Leiden, Holland: E.J. Brill, 1943), vol.2, p.387. See also *Sahih Muslim, vol.iv,pp.* 1348-9.

[94] Collected by ad-Daaraqutnee but 'Abdur-Rahmaan ibn Saalim is considered "Majhool (unknown)". Ibn Hajar, *Taqreeb at-Tahtheeb*, vol.1, p480.

Suwaid ibn Ghafalah[95] reported that once he passed by a group of Shee'ah who were talking about Abu Bakr and 'Umar in derogatory terms. Then he visited 'Alee ibn Abee Taalib and told him, "O Ameer al-Mu-mineen, I passed by a group of your companions while they were referring to Abu Bakr and 'Umar in derogatory terms. If it were not that they thought that you secretly felt as they openly said, they would not have dared to say it" 'Alee replied," I seek refuge in Allaah! I seek refuge in Allaah from secretly feeling anything towards the two of them other than what the Prophet (ﷺ) entrusted to me. May Allaah curse anyone who holds inside himself anything but goodness and gratitude towards both of them. (They were like) two brothers to Allaah's Messenger, his two companions, his two assistants, may Allaah's mercy be on both of them."

Then 'Alee got up with tears in his eyes, holding on to my hand until he entered the masjid. Next he ascended the mimber[96] and sat at its top holding onto his beard and looking at it until the people gathered. After having made a brief but eloquent speech, he added, "What is wrong with those who make allegations about the two masters of Quraysh, the two fathers of the Muslims, allegations which I would never say or ever want to hear others say; and for which I may be punished. By He who split the seed and created the soul, only a pious believer loves them, and only a wretched sinner hates them. Those two who accompanied Allaah's Messenger, commanding all that is good and prohibiting all that is evil; who became angry with wrongdoers and punished them based on truth and honesty alone. In their rulings, they did not overstep the

---

[95] Suwaid was among the major scholars of the Taabi'oon. He accepted Islaam during the lifetime of the Prophet (ﷺ) but never met him. On the day that the Prophet (ﷺ) was being buried in Madeenah, Suwaid came to the city for the first time. He later settled in Kufah and died at the age of 130 in the year 700 CE. All the major books of Hadeeth have Hadeeth narrated by him. Ibn Hajar, *Taqreeb at-Tahtheeb,* vol.1, p. 341.

[96] Tiered pulpit found in the front of masjids and first adopted by the Prophet (ﷺ) himself.

opinions of Allaah's Messenger. In fact, their opinions always coincided with those of Allaah's Messenger and the believers were pleased with both of them throughout their respective caliphates.

The Messenger of Allaah (ﷺ) appointed Abu Bakr to lead the believers in their prayers for the last nine days of the Prophet's (ﷺ) life and he died without recalling him. The believers, subsequently, made him responsible for their affairs,and gave him their Zakaah.[97] They willingly pledged allegiance to him and I am the first person from Banu 'Abd al-Mu ṯṯalib to confirm his leadership. He disliked leadership and wished that one of us would take his place. By Allaah, he was the best of those who remained after the Prophet (ﷺ); the eldest,the kindest, and truly the most compassionate and pious. He was like angel Mikaaeel in his benevolence and Prophet Ibraaheem in his willingness to forgive and his dignified bearing. He took the path of the Prophet (ﷺ) and passed away on that path (may Allaah have mercy on him).

After Abu Bakr, 'Umar took command, and I was among those pleased with his appointment. He ruled according to the policy of Allaah's Messenger (ﷺ) and his companion, Abu Bakr, following their footsteps the way a young camel follows its mother. I swear by Allaah, he was kind and gentle with the weak, a champion of the cause of the oppressed and without any blame concerning Allaah's religion. Allaah manifested examples of the truth through him and made the truth a part of him to such a degree that we used to think that an angel was speaking with his tongue. Allaah made his conversion a strengthening factor for Islaam, and placed in the hearts of the hypocrites a fear of him and in the hearts of the believers love for him. Allaah's Messenger (ﷺ) compared him to angel Jibreel in his harshness towards the enemies of Islaam. So who among you can be compared to the two of them. May Allaah's mercy be on them, and may Allaah provide us with the ability to continue in their paths. Let whoever loves me, love them, for whoever does not

---

[97] Religious tax taken from the well-to-do and given to the poor.

love them has angered me, and I will have nothing to do with him. If I hear anymore derogatory talk about the two of them, I will punish the offenders severely. After today, whoever is brought before me will get the punishment of a slanderer. Verily, the best of this nation after its Prophet (ﷺ) is Abu Bakr and ‘Umar, may Allaah be pleased with them. Then Allaah knows best who is the best. I am saying this asking Allaah’s forgiveness for both you and myself.”

THE DEVIL'S DECEPTION OF THE BAATINEEYAH [98]

The Baatineeyah is a group who hides behind Islaam and leans towards the Shiite creed, though their beliefs and actions are in fact totally contrary to Islaam. The end result of their philosophy is the negation of the Creator; invalidation of Prophethood and worship; and the denial of the hereafter. They do not reveal that ideology in the beginning but instead claim that Allaah is real, that Muhammad is Allaah's Messenger, and that the religion of Islaam is genuine. However, they explain that these things have a secret aspect which is not obvious. In that way, Iblees played with them by making many sects and doctrines pleasing to them. Historically, they have been known by the following eight names:

1. The Baatineeyah

They were given this name because of their claim that the literal texts of the Qur'aan and the Hadeeths have inner meanings which are like the kernel of a nut in relation to its shell.[99] They say that the exterior of the texts delude the ignorant masses into seeing only beautiful pictures which to the intelligent few are mere symbols and signs pointing to hidden realities. Furthermore, according to them, whoever's mind refrains from becoming immersed in the hidden secrets of the inner realms, and is satisfied with the outer and obvious meanings of the texts is in fact chained by the obligations of the Sharee'ah. While he who advances to the inner knowledge is released from the obligations of Sharee'ah and relieved from its burden. They claim that this interpretation is the intended mean-

---

[98] The word Baatineeyah, referred to as the Baatinites, is derived from the word "baatin" which means the inside of a thing. The Baatinites are those who claim that the Sharee'ah (Divine Law) has a Thaahir (outer aspect) and a baatin (inner aspect). ('Abdus-Salaam Haroon, *al-Mu'jam al-Waseet*, (Egypt:'Ilmeeyah Press) vol.2, p.91).

[99] Abu Haamid al-Ghazzaalee, *Fadaaih al-Baatineeyah,* (Daar al-Qawmeeyah Press, 1964) p.11.

ing of the Quranic verse, "He (the Prophet) releases them from their heavy burdens and the chains which bound them."[100] Their actual intention is to cancel the requirements implied by beliefs embodied in Islamic religious texts and replace them with false concepts completely opposed to the Sharee'ah (divine law).

2. The Ismaa'eeleeyah [101]

They trace their origin back to Muhammad ibn Ismaa'eel ibn Ja'far whom they claim ended the inherited Shee'ah Imaamate by being the seventh Imaam.[102] They brought as proof the fact that

---

[100] Soorah al-Aa'raaf 7:157.

[101] Commonly called the Ismailis.

[102] Officially the Ismaa'eeleeyah came into existance as a sect of the Shee'ah on the death of Ismaa'eel (d.760) before his father Imaam Ja'far as-Saadiq (d.765). Ja'far had designated his eldest son, Ismaa'eel, as his successor but having learned of Isma'eel's addiction to drinking changed his decision in favour of his second son, Moosaa. The majority of the Shee'ah went along with the change and continued the Imaamate in Moosa al-Kaathim (d.799). But others, claiming that the Imaam, as an infallible being, was unaffected by drinking wine, remained loyal to Ismaa'eel. (Ibn Khaldoon, *al Muqaddamah,* - pp167-8). After the death of Imaam Muhammad ibn Ismaa'eel, a branch of the sect accepted the belief that he was the final Imaam who would return on the Last Day. This sect became known as the Sab'eeyah (Seveners). The other branch accepted one of Imaam Muhammad's sons as their Imaam and followed his appointed successors. As the Imaams lived in strict disguise, and even their names were concealed, there was not much difference between both branches which were rapidly increasing in Khuzistan and southern Mesopotamia. The split became complete about 893 CD. *(Encyclopedia of Islam, p. 179).*

'Abdullaah ibn Maymoon al-Qaddaah (d.825), of obscure origin, had practised as an ocultist (Qaddaah) in Ahwaaz before moving to Jerusalem, where he joined the latter branch of the Ismaa'eeleeyah and became one of its most famous missionaries and theoreticians during this period of concealment. From his headquarters in Basrah and later Salameeyah in northern Syria, Ibn Maymoon and his successors devised a secret society with grades of initiation and a Neo-Platonic interpretation of existence. Secret missionaries were then sent to all parts of the Muslim empire to spread their teachings. Towards the close of the 9th century the chief missionary, Abu 'Abdullaah al-Husayn ash-Shee'ee, a native of San'aa in

Yaman, proclaimed himself precursor of the Mahdee and introduced the new Ismaa'eelee Baatinee teachings among the Berbers of North Africa, which was at the time under Aghlabid rule. One of 'Abdullaah ibn Maymoon's descendents, Sa'eed ibn Husayn, was persuaded to leave his headquarters in Salameeyah to take charge of the movement in north-west Africa. Together they succeeded in destroying the century old Aghlabid Sunni dynasty. In 909CE Sa'eed was then proclaimed ruler under the title of Imaam 'Ubaydullah al-Mahdee and accepted as a descendant of Faatimah through al-Husayn and Ismaa'eel. During the Faatimid rule of Egypt missionaries did not openly preach Ismaa'eelee thought as the masses of Egyptians never accepted Shiite thought. The dynasty lasted until 1171 when Salaahud-Deen dethroned the last Faatimid Caliph.

During the rule of the sixth Faatimid Caliph, al-Haakim bin Amril-laah (996-1021), an Ismaa'eelee missionary by the name of ad-Darazee claimed that al-Haakim's death, ad-Darazee preached that he did not die and a new sect was born under the name of the Haakimeeyah, later called the Druzes. Ad-Darazee and his followers were forced to leave Egypt and settled around Damascus in the mountains of Hawran and Lebanon. (Mustafaa Ghaalib, *al-Harakaat,* pp. 184 and 242) On the death of the eighth Faatimid caliph, al-Mustansir (1035-94), his eldest son and original nominee, Nizaar, was deposed by his brother al-Musta'lee (1094-1101). With that the Ismaa'eeleeyah split into two new branches, the Musta'lians and Nizaaris. Al-Hasan as-Sabbaah became one of the most infamous proponents of the Nizaaris branch. With the collapse of the Faatimid dynasty, the Musta'lians transfered their religious center to Yaman, where it remained in obscurity for about 500 years. Missionaries carried it from Yaman to India and the religious center was transfered to Gujurat in the early 17th century where they became known as Bohoras. The Nizaaris community in Syria has continued till today though the last war with their ancient enemies the Nusayris, in 1919, caused them enormous losses in land and property, including almost all of their religious books. The Nizaaris found root in Persia but remained relatively concealed. However, their missionaries carried their doctrines to northern India (Punjab, Upper Sind and Kashmir.) They later moved south to Gujurat under the Persian missionary, Imaam Shaah, 'Abdur-Raheem ibn Kabeer ad-Deen, who succeeded in converting large numbers of Hindus there at the end of the 15th century. His son and successor, Noor Muhammad Shaah, later proclaimed himself Imaam, thus causing a split in the community. Its center is near Ahmadabad in Gujurat. The main body came to be known as Khojas, who became a wealthy trading community in Bombay, lower Sind, Gujurat, Zanzibar, and Kenya. Their leader is titled Aga Khan. (Encylopedia of *Islam*, pp.180-1, 256):

> In the 19th century a man by the name of Hasan-'Alee Shaah appeared in Iran, gathered some Ismailis around him and

there are seven heavens, seven earths, and seven days in a week, all of which indicate that the cycle of Imaams would end at the seventh.

Based on the principle of the cycle of seven, some of them claimed that the lineage of Abu Ja'far al-Man<u>s</u>oor went from al-'Abbaas to his son, 'Abdullah, to his son, 'Alee, to his son, Mu<u>h</u>ammad ibn 'Alee, to his son, Mu<u>h</u>ammad ibn 'Alee, to his son

---

led a revolt, which briefly threatened the state and the ruling Qaajaar family. However, the revolt ended in failure. British colonialists who had designs on the region during this period intervened to have <u>H</u>asan-'Alee Shaah released from prison on condition that he would be exiled from Iran. <u>H</u>asan-'Alee Shaah then went to Afghanistan which was at war with the British, but he was soon expelled from the country in 1842. He then went to Sindh, India and after touring the country settled in Bombay. There <u>H</u>asan-'Alee Shaah claimed that he was descendant of the Faa<u>t</u>imid Imaam Nizaar and the British rulers of India officially recognized him as the head of the Nizaari branch and gave him the title Aga Khan (sometimes written Agha Khan - originally Aaghaa Khaan) which was a title bestowed on some of their nobles by the Qaajaar family. He succeeded in bringing back to life the Nizaari branch of the Ismaa'eeleeyah and organizing it after its virtual disappearance five centuries before. On his death in 1881 his son, Aga Khan II 'Alee Shaah became the new Imaam and ruled the sect until his death in 1883. He was succeeded by his eight year old son, Mu<u>h</u>ammad al- <u>H</u>usainee Aga Khan III. However, his mother, Lady 'Alee Shaah ran the the affairs of the sect until 1893 when she turned it over to him. In 1898 Aga Khan III travelled to Europe and decided to settle there, visiting his followers in India and Africa from time to time. He married a number of European wives and had two sons, 'Alee Sulaymaan Khan and Sadr ad-Deen Khan. 'Alee Sulayman also married a number of western women and his son, Kareem, by a Biritish wife, has become the present Aga Khan IV. (Mu<u>h</u>ammad Kaamil <u>H</u>asan, *<u>T</u>aaifah al-Ismaa'eeleeyah,* (Egypt: an-Nah<u>d</u>ah al-Mi<u>s</u>reeyah Press, 1st.ed., 1959, pp.41-50, 110-20. See also *Encyclopedia of Islaam pp.236-7.)* Yasmin Aga Khan is 'Alee Sulaymaan's daughter by actress Rita Hayworth, who recently married Basil Embiricos, Greek economist and shipping heir. *(Time Magazine,* vol. 125, no.21, May 27, 1985, p.36).

Ibraaheem, then to as-Saffaah then to al-Mansoor.

Abu Ja'far at-Tabaree mentioned in his history book[103] that 'Alee ibn Muhammad reported from his father that one day a leper, called al-Ablaq from ar-Raawand, cried out in a loud voice and began to invite the people of Khurasan to follow him. He claimed that the same spirit which was in 'Eesaa ibn Maryam was present in 'Alee ibn Abee Taalib, then in the Imaams, one after the other until it appeared in Ibraaheem ibn 'Alee, grandfather of 'Abbaasid Caliph, Abu Ja'far al-Man soor.

This branch of the Ismaa'eeleeyah made allowable practices forbidden by the Sharee'ah to such a degree that a man among them would invite a group to his house, feed them and give them drink, then give them his wife. When news of such practices reached Asad ibn 'Abdillaah, he ordered that those involved be executed and crucified. However, such practices continue among them to this day. They also worshipped Abu Ja'far and would ascend al-Khadra and hurl themselves off as if they were flying, but all would die upon striking the ground. A group of them rose in armed revolt, attacking people indiscriminately, shouting, "O Ja'far! You are God."[104]

3. The Sab'eeyah (The Seveners)

"This title was given to them because they believed that the Imaamate existed in infinite cycles of seven and that the meaning of the term Resurrection was the appearance of the seventh Imaam who ended his own cycle of seven. The title was also given based on their claim that the regulation of the lower world was entrusted

[103] Abu Ja'far Muhammad ibn Jareer at-Tabaree's book was entitled *Taareekh al-Umam wal-Mulook.*

[104] A Persian sect of extremists called the Raawandeeyah were mercilessly crushed by the forces of Caliph al-Mansoor (754-775) in the year 758CE (*Taareekh al-Umam wal-Mulook, vol.9,* pp.173-5)

to the seven astral spheres: Saturn, Jupiter, Mars, Venus, the Sun, Mercury, and the Moon."[105]

4. The Baabakeeyah

"This name was given to a group among them who followed a man from the Baatineeyah called Baabak al-Khurramee. He was born an illegitimate child but from his first appearance in the mountains near Adharbaijaan[106] in 817 CE, a number of people immediately began to follow him."[107] Soon his ideas began to spread rapidly, because he made many of the prohibited things lawful. If he found out that anyone had a beautiful daughter, he would demand her, and if his demand was not obeyed, he would kill her father and take her. He continued to function in this way for over twenty years during which time he and his followers massacred between eighty and two hundred and fifty-five thousand people. The authorities fought him, but their forces were continually defeated until Caliph al-Mu'tasim sent Afseen,[108] who fought and defeated them and brought Baabak and his brother before the Caliph in the year 838 CE. When they entered, Baabak's brother said to him, "You know what no one knows so patiently bear now what no one has borne." Baabak replied, "You will see my self-control." When al-Mu'tasim ordered that both of Baabak's hands and legs be chopped off, he wiped blood on his own face. Al-Mu'tasim then said to him, "You are well-known for your bravery, so why have you wiped blood on your face? Is it out of apprehension for your impending death?"

---

[105] The quote is from *Fadaaih al-Baatineeyah, p.16*
According to other sources previously mentioned, the Sab'eeyah were in fact a branch of Ismaa'eeleeyah which appeared after the death of Imaam Muhammad ibn Ismaa'eel. They considered him the final Imaam, the seventh, who would return on the Last Day. Later on towards the close of the 9th century, they came to be called the Qaraamitah after their leader, Hamdaan Qirmit.

[106] Azerbaijan - Constituent republic of the U.S.S.R. in east Transcaucasia bordering on the Caspian Sea.

[107] *Fadaaih al-Baatineeyah. p.14*

[108] Al-Afsheen is the correct spelling of the Turkish general's name.

Baabak replied, "No. When you cut off my limbs, I began to bleed and feared that it be said that my face became pale out of fear of death, so I covered my face with blood." Following that his head was chopped off and his body set on fire, and the same was done to his brother. Not a scream nor moan was heard from either of them, nor did they display any signs of fear.

"There remained a group from the Baabakeeyah which kept alive Baabak's philosophy of libertinism. It is said that they had one night every year in which their men and women would gather and extinguish the lamps. In the darkness the men would jump up, rush forward and grab any woman they could claiming that whoever caught hold of a woman could have sex with her based on the principle of the hunt which is allowable."[109]

5. The Mu<u>h</u>ammarah (Reddened Ones)

During Baabak's reign of terror and corruption, his followers used to wear clothes that were dyed red.[110]

6. The Qaraamitah

Muslim historians are of two opinions as to the origins of this title. One opinion holds that a man from the region of Khoozastaan[111] came among the people of Kufah, put on a show of piety and asceticism and called people to an Imaam from the Prophet's descendents. He stayed with a man nicknamed Kirmeetah, which in the Nabatean language means sharp-eyed, because his eyes were always red. One day he was placed under house arrest. While the governor slept with the key to the house under his pillow, a slave girl who felt sorry for the stranger stole the key, set him free, and re-

---

[109] This is their interpretation of verse 2 of Soorah al-Maidah 5:3 in which Allaah makes the hunting of animals allowable, "But when you are clear of the sacred precincts (Makkah) and the pilgrim garb, you may hunt..." See *Fa<u>d</u>aai<u>h</u> al-Ba<u>t</u>ineeyah,* p.15 for the quote.

[110] *Faa<u>d</u>aai<u>h</u> al-Baa<u>t</u>ineeyah, p.17*

[111] Khuzistan is a region of SW Iran corresponding to ancient Elam.

turned it. When the governor ordered that the captive be brought to him, he was nowhere to be found.This incident caused the masses to become even more intrigued and attracted to him. He then went to Syria and called himself Kirmeetah after the one in whose house he had stayed; later shortening it to Qirmit. His family and children later inherited his position and name.

The other opinion is that the sect[112] "was named after one of the early Ismaa'eelee propagandists called H̲amdaan Qirmit. A number of people responded to his call and were subsequently named Qaraamitah or Qirmiteeyah. He was from the city of Kufah and inclined toward asceticism. One day H̲amdaan met a Baat̲inee missionary when he was with a group herding some cows toward a village. When H̲amdaan found out they were going to the same village, he told the missionary to ride one of the cows. The missionary replied that he could only do as ordered.When H̲amdaan asked whose orders he obeyed, the missionary replied that it was by the command of his Owner and Hamdaan's Owner, the Owner of this world and the next. Then Hamdaan said that it was Allaah, the Lord of the worlds, and the man replied that he had spoken the truth. Next H̲amdaan found out that the missionary had been commanded to call the village people from ignorance to knowledge, from a state of misguidance to guidance, and from wretchedness to happiness; to save them from their plight of humiliation, disgrace, and poverty; and to give them what would suffice them from their toil. H̲amdaan then begged the missionary to save him by giving him the knowledge, because he was in great need of it. However, the missionary told him that he was not allowed to reveal the hidden secret to anyone except after being sure about his commitment and after taking an oath of allegiance from him. H̲amdaan asked him to inform him of the oath and promised to abide by it. The missionary told him to make an oath and covenant by Allaah to him and to the

---

[112] The quotation marks are mine. The following passage was taken verbatim from al-Ghazaalee's book *Fad̲aaih̲ al-Baat̲ineeyah, pp.12-14.*

Imaam not to reveal either the secret of the Imaam or his own personal secret. When Hamdaan made the oath, the missionary began to teach him little by little until he ensnared him and won him over to the sect. Hamdaan was then appointed as a missionary and became one of the chief figures of the Ismaa'eelee sect."[113]

Subsequently, his family and sons inherited his favoured position and rank. Perhaps the most brutal of his descendants was Abu Sa'eed, who surfaced in the year 899CE.[114] He managed to swiftly gather around himself a powerful fighting force which murdered countless Muslims including even pilgrims on their way to or from Makkah. They also destroyed many masjids and burned numerous copies of the Qur'aan. On his death, his followers built a dome over his grave and put a bird made of plaster on top of it, claiming that if the bird flew away, Abu Sa'eed had risen from the grave. They also placed a horse, a robe of honor, and weapons near his tomb. Iblees further seduced this group into believing that whoever dies among them, while owning a horse will be resurrected riding and if he does not own a horse, he will be resurrected walking.

Abu Sa'eed's followers used to invoke Allaah's peace and blessings on him whenever they mentioned his name, but not when

---

[113] About 890 the founder built himself an official residence, Daar al-Hijrah (refuge for emigrants) near Kufah, which became the headquarters of the new movement. Active propaganda among the native masses, especially the Nabataean peasants and artisans, as well as among the Arabs themselves, swelled the numbers of members in the new sect. Fundamentally, the organization was a secret society based on a system of communism in which Qirmit went so far as to prescribe not only that property be communally owned but also wives. They organized workers and artisans into trade guilds which in the opinion of the French orientalist Maisignon reached the West and influenced the fromation of European guilds and Freemasonry. *(History of the Arabs, pp. 444-5)*

[114] Abu Sa'eed al-Hasan al-Jannaabee. Jannaab was a town in Persia near the mouth of a river emptying into the Persian Gulf. In the same year he succeeded in establishing an independant state on the western shore of the Persian Gulf with al-Ahsaa as its capital (modern al-Hufoof). *(Al-Kaamil fee at-Taareekh,* Ibn al-Atheer, vol.8, p.63).

they mentioned the Prophet's (ﷺ) name. And, if they heard anyone invoke Allaah's peace and blessings on the Prophet (ﷺ) they would say, "Are you eating Abu Sa'eed's provision and invoking blessings on Abul Qaasim?[115] "He appointed as his successor his son, Abu Taahir,[116] who let loose a reign of terror similar to that of his father. An attack on the very Ka'bah was mounted in which he tore down the door and seized the relics inside it. Then he removed the Black Stone from its position in the corner of the Ka'bah and carried it away to his country claiming that he was Allaah in person.[117]

7. The Khurrameeyah

The word Khurram is a Persian word which refers to something desirable and pleasing. This title used to be given to the Mazdak sect among the Zoroastrians which appeared during the era of Qabaadh and adopted a libertine attitude of free sex with no prohibitions. Since the Ismaa'eeleeyah enticed people to follow their desires and urges, removed all their responsibilities; and dropped the laws of the Sharee'ah much in the same way as the Mazdakians did, they were also given this title.[118]

---

[115] The title adopted by Prophet Muhammad (ﷺ)

[116] Abu Taahir Sulaymaan laid waste most of lower Iraq and cut the pilgrim routes. (*Al-Kaamil fee at-Taareekh,* Ibn al-Atheer, vol.8, pp.124-5)

[117] During this attack, pilgrims were massacred and their bodies thrown in the well of Zamzam and the Black Stone remained in their headquarters in Ahsaa (Eastern Arabia) for 23 years until the Faatimid Caliph, al-Mansoor, who was himself an Ismaa'eelee, ordered them to return it to Makkah. (*Al-Kaamil,* Ibn al-Atheer, vol.8, pp 153-4)

[118] According to Mutahhar ibn Taahir, who met members of the community, they hold the belief that revelation never ceases and every adherent of a religion is in the right, so long as he hopes for reward and fears punishment. They had Imaams to whom they had recourse in legal matters, and apostles who would accompany them on their raids and whom they called by the Persian name (firishtah: Angel). Wines and liquors were, in their opinion, more fortune bringing than all other things. They permitted promiscuity where the women consented and the enjoyment of anything craved by the natural mind, provided no injury resulted. *(Ency-*

8. The Ta'leemeeyah

"This title was given to them because of their fundamental principle of denying the validity of opinion or reason and their inviting people to the teachings (Ar. Ta'leem) of the infallible Imaam, because knowledge is only achieved through teaching."[119]

Their strategy

The Baatineeyah have a particular technique for luring and seducing the masses. First, they distinguish between those who may be ensnared and those who are desperate. When they detect a potential follower, they closely observe his nature. If he leans towards asceticism, they invite him to honesty, truth, and the abandonment of desires. On the other hand, if he leans toward licentiousness, they propose that the performance of the rites of worship is idiotic, that piety is foolishness, and that astuteness lies in seeking the pleasures of this life. That is, they first confirm the beliefs of whatever sect or school or thought the potential follower subscribes to, then they create doubts in the mind of the subject about his beliefs.[120]

---

clopedia of Islam, pp.257-8)

According to Mas'oodee, *Murooj al-Thahab,* vi, 186, they came into prominence after the execution of Abu Muslim of Khurasan in 755, but while some of them denied that he was dead and foretold his return "to spread justice in the world", others maintained the Imaamate of his daughter Faatimah, and were labeled the Muslimeeyah and the Faatimeeyah. One by the name Sambaath started a rebellion in Khurasan demanding vengeance for Abu Muslim, but this was suppressed within seventy days. They were next heard of in the reign of caliph al-Ma-moon when Baabak rebelled against the government and entrenched himself in Bathth, a village between Atharbaijan and Arran. He maintained himself there and unleased a reign of terror from 817 till 838 CE. *(Encylopedia of Islam, p.257, Fadaaih al-Baatineeyah, p.14)*

[119] A direct quote from *Fadaaih al-Baatineeyah*, p.17

[120] Quietly and cautiously the novice was initiated under oath of secrecy in the esoteric doctrines, including such concealed ones as the formation of the universe by emanation from the divine essence, transmigration of souls, the manifestations of the divinity in Ismaa'eel and the expectation of his early return (raj'ah) as the Mahdee. Initiation is said to have involved seven to nine graded stages which recall modern Freemasonry.

Those who respond to their call are usually of the following types:

(a) Foolish and ignorant individuals,

(b) Descendents of the Khosraus (Persian kings), whose empire was cut short by the Islamic states,

(c) Children of Zoroastrians, who never accepted Islaam, but kept their religious beliefs alive.

(d) One who desires mastery and control over others but was unsuccessful,

(e) The haughty individual who seeks hidden knowledge to confirm his intellectual superiority over the masses.

(f) Shee'ah who consider cursing the companions of the Prophet (ﷺ) a religious duty.

(g) Atheist philosophers

(h) One who is confused about his religion,

(i) The morally deprived who are overwhelmed by their desires and who find the tenets of religion burdensome.

Their Beliefs

Abu Haamid at-Toosee[121] stated that among the principles of the Baatineeyah is the belief in two Gods, both without beginning in time, yet one is the reason for the other's existence. The Saabiq (the former or the one which precedes) is not described in terms of existence or non-existence, because it neither exists nor does not exist, it is neither known nor unknown, neither describable nor undescribable.In addition, from the former emanated the latter, who is the first creator and then in another emanation, the universal

---

[121] Abu Haamid Muhammad ibn Muhammad at-Toosee (1058-1111CE) was more commonly known as "al-Ghazzaalee". He was born in Toos and was educated there as well as at Naisabur. From Naisabur he went to the court of Nithaam al-Mulk, the Salijuq Wazeer and formed a part of his retinue of legists and theologians until 1091 when he was appointed to teach in the Nithaameeyah Madrasah at Baghdad. There he taught and wrote law according to the Shaafa'ee Math-hab. He also wrote books against the Baatinites, among them *Fadaaih al-Baaatineeyah.*

soul came into being. According to them, the Prophet (ﷺ) is one on whom the former (Saabiq) by way of the latter emanates a holy and pure force. Jibreel, on the other hand, is considered merely the intelligence which was emanated on the Prophet (ﷺ) and not an individual per se.

They all agree that every age must have an Imaam, whose infallibility equals that of the Prophet (ﷺ) and on whom the interpretation of all things depends. They deny the next life claiming that it merely represents the return of things to their origin. As for religious obligations, they are known for their unrestricted licentiousness; however, when confronted with this position, they deny it and instead confirm the necessity of obligations and restrictions for all humankind.[122]

Since they were unable to divert people from the Qur'aan and the Sunnah, they diverted people from their real menages to strange misconceptions which they elaborately concocted. For, if they had openly denied the Qur'aan and Sunnah, they would have been summarily executed. For example they claimed that the meaning of Janaabah[123] was the premature revelation of secrets to one who has responded to their call. And, Ghusl[124] to them meant renewal of one's covenant if one prematurely revealed the sect's secrets. Zinaa (fornication) meant casting a drop of inner knowledge into a soul who has not yet taken his oath. Similarly, S̲iyaam (fasting) came to mean abstinence from the revelation of secrets. The Ka'bah was the Prophet (ﷺ) himself and the Baab (door) was 'Alee ibn Abee Taalib. The Flood was the flood of knowledge which drowns those who adhere to doubtful ideas and the Ark, the amulet, which protects one who responds to the call. The fire in which the Prophet Ibraaheem was thrown refers to Nimrod's anger and not a real fire. Is-h̲aaq's sacrifice was the taking of the oath from him,

---

[122] al-Ghazzaalee, *Fad̲aaih̲ al-Baat̲ineeyah,* pp.38-54.

[123] The state of impurity produced by sex or wet dreams.

[124] A complete bath which is taken if one enters a state of Janaabah to obtain a state of purity (Tahaarah) necessary for certain religious acts like formal prayer (S̲alaah).

and Prophet Moosaa's staff was his convincing arguments. The Gog and Magog are those who follow the outer and obvious meanings of the religion.[125]

Others besides Abu Haamid have narrated that they claim that when Allaah created the souls, He appeared among them as one of them and the first ones to recognize Him were Salmaan al-Faarisee, al-Miqdaad, and Abu Tharr. While the first to deny him was 'Umar ibn al-Khattaab under the name Iblees. They have countless other fables which are not worth mentioning. People like these do not adhere to any legal point about which a debate may take place. They simply invent ideas and concepts according to the circumstances they find themselves in.

Their Revival

The ember of the latter day Baatineeyah was re-ignited in 1101. In that year Sultaan Jalaal ad-Dawlah Barqiyaaruq[126] (1094-1104) killed over three hundred of their descendants when their deviations were accidentally discovered and exposed. Their wealth and properties were investigated and it was discovered that one of them had over seventy houses of engraved stone. When a report to that effect was sent to the Caliph, and an order was issued for the arrest of anyone suspected of belonging to the sect, no one dared to intercede on behalf of anyone else for fear that he also would be suspect of such leanings. Suspicion and accusation spread among the masses like wild-fire; whereby, anyone who disliked someone would accuse him of being a Baatinee, drag him away and snatch his wealth.

---

[125] al-Ghazzaalee, *Fadaaih al-Baatineeyah,* pp.55-8.

[126] He was Sultaan under the 'Abbaasid Caliph, al-Mustath-hir, (1094-1118) as Malik Shaah's second successor and son, (Philip Hitti, *History of the Arabs,* Macmillan Press, London, 6th ed. 1958 p.480, from Ibn Khallikaan, vol.1,p.154).

However, in later times the first record of the Baatineeyah occurred during the reign of Jalaal ad-Deen Malik Shaah (1072-1092)[128] when a group of them gathered together to pray Salaah al-'Eid in Saawah. The police became aware of their gathering and arrested a number of them, but later set them free. They tried to entice the muath- thin of Saawah into the sect, but he rejected their advances, so they killed him fearing that he might inform on them. When the news reached Nithaam al-Mulk (1063-1092CE),[129] he had the carpenter who was accused of the murder executed. Consequently their first political assassination was that of Nithaam al-Mulk. They used to say, "You killed a carpenter from among us, and we killed Nithaam al-Mulk in retaliation." They began to spread dangerously in Isfahan and by the time that Malik Shaah died they were kidnapping people, killing them, and throwing their bodies in the local well. If the time of 'Asr neared and someone had not returned home, his family gave up all hope of finding him alive.

Eventually, the people of Isfahan took it upon themselves to make a house to house search throughout the city for a solution to the kidnappings and murders. After some time they found a woman in a house who refused to move off a mat. When they forcibly removed her, they found 40 corpses buried under it. So they killed her and burned down her house and the neighbourhood in which she lived.

Later on they found out the scheme used on her victims.A blind man used to sit near the entrance of the alley where her house was located and when someone passed by, he would ask the person to lead him a few steps to the alley. When they reached the alley, people from the house would grab him then drag him into the house and overpower him. Following this incident other people of Isfahan diligently hunted down other followers of the sect and killed a large

---

128 Sultaan, who ran the 'Abbaasid state of Caliph al-Muqtadee (1075-1094) and under whom Saljooq's power reached its peak. *(History of the Arabs, p.476)*

129 Wazeer (vice-regent) during the reign of the Saljooq Sultaans, Alp Arslaan and Malik Shaah.

number of them.

The first fortress which the Baatineeyah possessed belonged to a grain merchant friend of Sultaan Malik Shaah living in a region of Dailam called Roozabaad.[130] Al- Hasan ibn as- Sabbaah from the city of Marw and a former scribe of its mayor, and ‘Abdur-‘Razzaaq ibn Bahraam paid a Baatinee guarding the fortress 1,200 Deenars to turn it over to them. As- Sabbaa h and his followers occupied the fortress in the year 1091 during Sultaan Malik Shaah's rule. As a young man, As- Sabbaah had travelled to Egypt, where he met and studied under Baatinee missionaries. Some years later he returned to his native land, a missionary and a leader among the Baatineeyah.[131]

After acquiring the fortress, his basic principle in calling others was to only invite people so ignorant that they could not distinguish between their left and their right, those who had no knowledge or experience in life. He would feed potential followers walnuts, honey and black caraway[132] until they were perfectly relaxed, then the oppression and injustice meted out to the Prophet's descendents would be mentioned to them in vivid detail until feelings

---

[130] Other sources refer to the first mountain fortress which was acquired as Alamoot, northwest of Qazween. It was strategically situated on an extension of the Alburz mountain chain, 10,200 feet above sea-level between the shores of the Caspian Sea and the Persian highlands. This "eagle's nest" as the name probably means, gave the Grand Masters of the Assassins a central stronghold of primary importance. Its possession represents the first historical fact in the life of the new order. *(History of the Arabs, p.446)*

[131] Al-Hasan was commissioned by the chief Baatinee missionary in Perisa, Ibn ‘Attaash in 1072 to go to Cairo to the Faatimid Caliph, al-Mustansir. In 1078 he arrived there after first travelling through Persia, Mesopotamia and Syria. In the struggle as to who was to succeed the aged ruler, he took the side of Nizaar, while others preferred another of Mustansir's sons, who actually occupied the Egyptian throne on his father's death under the name al-Musta‘lee. He then returned to the East and advocated Nizaar's cause in different places. *(Encylopedia of Islam, p.136)*

[132] The Arabic word is "shooneez" which is more commonly know as "habbah saudaa" (Nigella Sativa l., bot.)

of anguish and disgust overwhelmed them. Next he would ask them how it was that the Azaariqah[133] and the Khaarijites so willingly sacrificed their lives in fighting the Umayyads, yet they, the Shee'ah, were so unwilling to come to the aid of their Imaam. They then would be left with that thought to arouse their feelings of guilt and incite them to fight.[134]

When Ibn as-Sabbaah's followers began to threaten the security of the state by assassinating scholars and governors, Malik Shaah sent a messenger to demand his obedience and threaten him if he refused.[135] He told the messenger that he would show him his an-

---

[133] The most dangerous of the Khaarijite sects to threaten the unity of the Muslims Empire. Under its founder Naafi'ibn al-Azraq, it gained control of Kirmaan, Faars and other eastern provinces and constituted a permanent threat to the security of Basrah and the surrounding country. They were not overcome until 699CE after years of effort which ended in the defeat and death of the last of the Azraqee leaders, Qataree ibn al-Fujaa-a at the hands of al-Hajjaaj ibn Yousuf. *(Encyclopedia of Islam, pp.247)* see p. 22 also.

[134] Al-Hasan and his followers came to be known as the Assassins, the rendering of the French chroniclers on the Crusades since the 12th century of the Arabic word Hash-shaasheen (consumers of Hasheesh). *(Encylopedia of Islam, p.48)*

[135] One of the first victims was the famous Wazeer Nithaam al-Mulk in 1092. The death of Sultaan Malik Shaah which occurred soon after and the resulting disputes for the successor among various claimants, and the appearance soon after of the Crusaders in the lands of Islaam threw the Muslim world into a disorder which assured great success to the Assassins. Their strength consequently became very considerable in a few years, until the Saljooq Sultaan, Muhammad I ascended the throne and threw all of his forces into combatting the Assassins. The fortress of Dizkooh, called Shaah-Diz after Malik Shaah, in the vicinity of Isfahan was at that time in the hands of Ibn 'Attaash. It was captured after a fierce resistance in 1107 and the Turkish Ameer Anushtefeen Sheergeer was then entrusted with the conduct of the war against the Assassins. After several successes, he was on the point of taking the fortress of Alamoot itself when the death of Muhammad I (1118CE) forced him to raise the siege. Al-Hasan survived this danger almost seven years. He died in 1124 leaving the leadership of the Assassins to Kiaya Buzung Ummend Roodbaaree (1124-1138) who bequeathed the conduct of affairs to his descendants. During the rule of these Grand-Masters more than once the Assassins had to endure attempts to eradicate them, but neither the Caliphs nor the Salijooq Sultaans succeeded in breaking their power and destroying their nests of corruption. They

swer, and said to a group of his followers sitting near him, "I would like to save you by sending you to your Lord on an assignment, so who is ready?" All of them craned their necks anxiously to be chosen. The Sultaan's messenger supposed that Ibn as-Sabbaah was referring to a letter he wanted them to take back to Malik Shaah. Ibn as-Sabbaah then nodded his head to one young man who quickly jumped up, and told him to kill himself. He obediently pulled out a dagger, stabbed himself in the adam's apple, and dropped dead. He then told another man to hurl himself from the walls of the fortress which he promptly did, dashing himself on the rocks below. Ibn as-Sabbaah then turned to the Sultaan's messenger and said, "Tell your leader that I have with me twenty thousand others as obedient to me as they are. That is my answer."

---

skillfully ridded themselves of their most implacable enemies by assassination and zealously carried on their propaganda. They succeeded in gaining an especially firm foothold in Syria where the Saljooq of Halab Ridwaan, sought their aid. Abu Taahir as-Saaigh was subsequently sent to Syria as an emissary and won many followers, particularly in Halab. In 1105 he managed by treachery to clear the governor of Apamea out of the way, but his hopes of becoming master of the town were dashed as the Crusaders soon after took possession of it. Some years later another Persian emissary named Bahrram succeeded in obtaining a large following and gaining possession of the town of Baaniyaas (1126) which was surrendered three years later to the Crusaders. The Assassins often entered into friendly relations with the Christians, and continued to strengthen their position by cleverly availing themselves of the political conditions. In 1140, they conquered the hill-fortress of Masayaaf and other fortresses situated in north Syria.

The Mongols who effected such great changes in the political conditions of Asia, accomplished also the downfall of the Assasins. The last Grand master, Rukn ad-Deen, had just stepped into office when Hulagu marched his forces on Alamoot. Resistance was impossible as Rukn ad-Deen had to submit (1256) and was executed. The strongholds of the Assassins were taken and some of them razed to the ground. The hill-fortresses of Syria fell in 1260 under the thrust of the Mongols, but the finishing blow was given to the Assasins by Mamlook Sultaan Baibars in 1271. This ended forever the political power of the dreaded sect. *(Encylopedia. of Islam, pp.48-9)*

When the messenger returned to Sultaan Malik Shaah and informed him of what had transpired, Malik Shaah was so astonished that he decided to leave them alone after that. As a result, many other fortresses fell to al- Hasan ibn as-Sabbaah and his followers and they assassinated many provincial governors and ministers of the ‘Abbaasid state.

BIBLIOGRAPHY

Arabic

'Abdul-Baaqee, Muhammad, *al-Mu'jam al-Mufahras li Alfaath al-Qur'aan,* (Cairo: Daar ash-Sha'b Press)

Abu Zahrah, Muhammad, *Taareekh al-Mathaahib al-Islaameeyah,* (Cairo: Daar al-Fikr al-'Arabee), 2 vols.

al-'Ajloonee, Ismaa'eel, *Kashf al-Khafaa,* (Beirut: ar-Risaalah Establishment, 2nd ed., 1979) 2 vols.

al-Ash'aree, Abdul-Hasan, *Maqaalaat al-Islaameeyeen,* (Cairo: Maktabah an-Nahdah al-Misreeyah, 2nd. ed., 1969), 2 vols.

al-Baghdaadee, 'Abdul-Qaahir, *al-Farq bain al-Firaq,* (Beirut: Daar al Mar'rifah)

Bek, Muhammad al-Khadaree, *Itmaam al-Wafaa,* (Egypt: al-Maktabah at-Tajaareeyah al-Kubraa, 9th. ed., 1964)

ath-Thahabee, Muhammad, *Meezaan al-I'tidaal,* (Egypt: Daar Ihyaa al-Kutub al-'Arabeeyah, 1st.ed., 1963), 4 vols.

Ghaalib, Mustafaa, *al-Harakaat at-Baatineeyah fee al-Islaam* (Beirut: Daar al-Kaatib al-'Arabee)

al-Ghazzaalee, Abu Haamid, *Fadaaih al-Baatineeyah,* (Kuwait Daar al-Kutub ath-Thaqaafeeyah)

Haaroon, 'Abdus-Salaam, *al-Mu'jam al-Waseet,* (Tehraan: al-Maktabah al-'Ilmeeyah), 2 vols.

Tah-theeb Seerah Ibn Hishaam
(Beirut: al-Maktabah al-Umaweeyah, 1972), 2 vols.

Hasan, Muhammad Kaamil, *Taaifah al-Ismaa'eeleeyah,* (Egypt: an-Nahdah al-Misreeyah Press, 1st ed., 1959)

Ibn al-Atheer, 'Alee, *al-Kaamil fee at-Taareekh,* (Beirut: Daar Saadir Press, 1967)

an-Nihaayah fee Ghareeb al-Hadeeth wal-Aathaar (Beirut: al-Maktabah al-Islaameeyah, 1st. ed., 1963), 5 vols.